Fifth Grade

LET'S TAKE A TRIP TO A FISHERY

Let's take a trip to a

FISHERY

by Sarah R. Riedman

 ABELARD-SCHUMAN

NEW YORK

Contents

1   Visit to a Fish Pier   11

From Sea to Plate   11
Out on the Pier   12
The Fleet Is In   18
"Glad to Have You Aboard"   20
"Home" for the Fisherman   24
What a Catch!   28
An Icy Bed   31
You Name the Fish   32
Not for Fun   33

2   Brave Men   36

Far Away and Long Ago   36
Fish—and the Pilgrims   37
The Sacred Cod   38
Will My Ship Come In?   40
The Gloucester Fisherman   41

3   Bringing in the Catch   46

Fish Maps   46
North, South, East, West   47
Fish Biographies   52
Schools of Fish   56
Water Highways   59

4   All Kinds of Gear   64

Hook, Line, and Sinker   64
Fish in Traps   68
Come into My Parlor   72
Caught in a Purse   75
Dragging the Ocean Bottom   77
Tangled in a Net   79

5   The Fish-Pier Market   80

While the City Sleeps   80
How Much Am I Bid?   80
De-Icing and Washing   83
The Fish Gets a Shave   85
Which Fish is Fresh?   86
Fillet Means "No Bones"   87
Dressed Up in Cellophane   90
A Quick Trip   91
Barrels of Left-Overs   92

6   How to Keep a Fish   93

The Left-over Catch   93
Fish in a Factory   94
Hanging Up to Dry   95
That Smoky Taste   97
Salting to Keep   98
Fish Cakes by the Ton   100
Enter Canned Fish   101
Frozen on a Shelf   102
The Newest Taste   105

7   Sea Food—But Not Fish   108

Oysters—In Season and Out   108
Oyster Time   111
Shucking Oysters   112
Tested Clams   113

8   The Fish You Don't Eat   115

Fish for Bait   115
More Mink Coats   116
Chickens on a Fish Pier   117
From Ocean to Soil   118
A Hundred Uses   119
Sticky Stuff   119
Vitamins for Baby   120

9   Fish in the Future   122

New Ways of Fishing   122
Fish Science   123
S.O.S. for Fish   124
More Fish to Eat   126

Illustrations

Boston Fish Pier	10	The continental shelf	
Fish piers	12, 13	and banks	50-51
Hosing down the pier	14	Cod	53
Weighing the fish	14	Haddock	54
Refueling	14	Herring	54
Calking the hull	14	Mackerel	54
Mending nets	15	Menhaden	58
Nets drying	15, 16	Striped bass	59
Seagulls eating gurry	17	Swordfish	59
Loading fish on hand		Brook trout	60
trucks	17	King Salmon	60
Diesel-engined dragger	18	Sea mussel	61
Schooner	19	Bay scallop	61
Winch raising metal basket		Blue crab	61
filled with oysters	21	Lobster	62
Lowering the trawler	22	Lures	65
Harpooning	23	Line trawl	66
Trawler net filled with fish	25	Weir	68
Buoys to spread nets	25	Alewife	69
Forecastle	26	Fishing with pound nets	70
Crew's quarters	27	Pile trap	71
Cleaning haddock on		Floating trap	71
board	30	Lobster pot	73
Ice on board	32	Eel traps	74, 75
Rosefish	33	Purse seine	76
Snow-covered fishing boat	34	Beam trawl	77
The "Sacred Cod"	39	Otter trawl	77
The "Widow's Walk"	41	Gill net	78
Room where *Captains*		Fulton Fish Market,	
Courageous was written	42	New York City	81
Statue of Gloucester		Auction room	81
fisherman	43	De-icer	83
Ceremony in memory of		Fish being washed on	
fishermen lost at sea	44	escalator	84
Fish map of the United		Hand electric shaver	85
States	48-49		

Descaling machine   85
Hand filleting   86-89
Automatic filleting
    machine   89
Packaging fillets   91
Fillets packed in tin boxes   91
Salmon drying on racks   94
Cod drying   95

Preparation of fish
    cakes   100, 101
Quick freezers   103
Preparation of fish
    sticks   106, 107
Tongs for oysters   109
Scallop rake   110
Fish ladder   125

ACKNOWLEDGMENTS

To all those who have helped immeasurably in gathering material for this book, and in presenting it more accurately to you, dear reader, the author wishes to give heartfelt thanks. To Gorton-Pew Fisheries Company, Ltd. for conducting the author through their plant in Gloucester and for the picture on page 34; and to Mr. L. J. Hart of the Gloucester Chamber of Commerce for arranging for the trip and for the loan of the photographs used on pages 12, 14 (lower right), 15 (upper), 16, 17 (top), and 91 (left); to Mr. Thomas D. Rice of the Massachusetts Fisheries Association, Inc., for photographs on pages 10, 17 (bottom), 26, 27, 71 (bottom), 78, 80 (lower right), 84, 91 (right), 95, 109, and 125; to Mr. Harry Schadt of Teddy's The House of Sea Food, Inc. (New York); to the Great Atlantic & Pacific Tea Co., National Fish Department (Boston) for a conducted tour of the respective processing plants; and to Mr. Joseph C. O'Brien of the latter company for photographs showing the processes on pages 89 (top), 100, 101, 103, 106 (right), and 107 (right); to Mr. Irwin Rosenthal, Boston Bonnie Fisheries, for permission to take photographs in that plant.

The author is deeply indebted to Mr. F. M. Bundy, President of Gorton-Pew Fisheries, to Mr. Rice, Executive Secretary of the Massachusetts Fisheries Association, and to Dr. James E. Morrow of Bingham Oceanographic Laboratory (New Haven) for their careful reading of the manuscript and valuable suggestions for corrections they made.

Many thanks also to Mr. J. Calvert Hudson, Chaplain, Gloucester Fishermen's Institute, for the pictures on pages 30, 42, 43, and 44; to Mrs. Gladys Sundell, Department of Commerce, Commonwealth of Massachusetts for the pictures on pages 39 and 66; to Standard Oil Co. (N. J.) picture library for pictures on pages 13, 14, 15 (lower), 19, 21, 22, 23, 25 (left), 81 (top and lower left); to the U. S. Fish and Wildlife Service for pictures on pages 33, 53, 54, 59, 60, 61, 62, 69, 70, 71 (top), 75, 86, 87, 88, 89, and 94; to Fairchild Aerial Surveys, Inc. for the picture on page 10; to Gulf Oil Company for pictures on pages 18 and 85 (center) which appeared in "Commercial Fishing"; to Bureau of Fisheries, Dep't. of Interior for pictures on pages 58 and 110; to Abercrombie & Fitch Co., New York, for pictures on page 65; to Massachusetts Dep't. of Nat'l. Resources, Division of Marine Fisheries for the picture on page 66; to Michigan Dep't. of Conservation, for picture on page 70; to the *Baltimore Sunday Sun* for picture on page 74, and to New England Trawler Equipment Co., for the picture on page 77. The pictures on pages 68, 73, and 76 originally appeared in "Fishery Resources of the U. S.," Congressional Document #51, Dep't. of Interior, and the maps on pages 48-49, 50-51 are adapted from maps which appeared in that publication.

To my husband, Elton T. Gustafson, I owe the suggestion that this "trip" be to a fishery, and acknowledgment for the pictures he took on the Boston and Gloucester fish piers which appear on pages 25 (right), 32, 41, 83, 85 (left and right), 106 (left), and 107 (left).

S.R.R.

Boston Fish Pier from the air

CHAPTER ONE

Visit to a Fish Pier

FROM SEA TO PLATE

Fish for dinner today!

That sounds simple, doesn't it? You go to the store and buy it. Then you bring it home and cook it. You eat it, and it tastes fine. That's all there is to it. Or is it?

What happened to the fish before it reached the store? Where did it come from? Who caught it? Who got it ready to be sold?

From the open ocean to your plate is a long journey; and many things happened to your fish along the way. As many as thirty people may have worked on it. Most of the work is done at the water's edge, at or near the pier where the fishing boats dock.

Let's visit a fish pier and see what's going on. The true story of what happened to your fish is the biggest "fish story" of all.

OUT ON THE PIER

If you live in a city near a large body of water, you can visit a fish pier. It may be on the Atlantic or Pacific coast, on the Great Lakes, or at the vast mouth of the Mississippi River. You could visit a pier in Boston or Gloucester, Massachusetts; in Norfolk, Virginia; in New Orleans, Louisiana; or in Seattle, Washington. We are going to visit a big pier on the Atlantic coast.

Along the waterfront at Gloucester, Mass. The small boats in front are seine boats; the larger boats in back are mackerel seiners

Shrimp fleet at Morgan City, Louisiana

We step on to the water-soaked planks. The boards are drenched, and the dock workers are wearing heavy boots or thick-soled rubbers. In fact, they tell you that you, too, should have rubbers to protect your shoes from the salt; it soaks into the leather and leaves "rotting" stains. Most of the water comes from the melted ice and salt in which the fish are packed on the boats. Some of the water comes from the hosing down, done by the workers to keep the pier clean (page 14).

Sturdy, white-painted fishing boats are coming in and going out. Some are tied up to the dock, where pier workers are unloading, inspecting, sorting, and weighing (page 14) the fish. Others are being outfitted, before shoving off on the next fishing run. Men are bringing fuel (page 14), food, water, salt, and ice for the trip, and the crews are cutting bait, calking the boat, splicing

cable, and mending masts and nets. Miles and miles of
nets, covered with tar, are hanging on large racks to dry
(pages 15 and 16).

Sea gulls crowd thickly around the boats, screaming
angrily as they swoop after scraps which have been
dumped into the water (page 17). The fishermen call
this fish waste *gurry*.

Hosing down the pier

Weighing the fish

Refueling

Calking the hull

Mending the nets

Tarred fishing nets spread out to dry in Louisiana

If you closed your eyes you would still know you are on a fish pier. You would smell the salty air and the fishy smell of the scraps. You would hear the sounds of the splashing water as the boats pulled in, and the voices of the men calling to each other as they tied the boats to the pier.

On the other side of the pier are large, low buildings

with wide doors opening on to the wharf. Haulers with hand trucks are rolling the fish over to this factory which has all kinds of machinery for cleaning, cutting, and packing the fish. Behind the buildings we catch sight of a line of trucks, waiting to carry the fresh fish to the markets. Rush, rush, rush, from boat to pier to buildings to trucks, for fresh fish spoil easily, and their trip to the market must take only a few hours.

Now let's go over to the edge of the wharf, and watch the fishing boats come in.

Drag nets hung up to dry and to be repaired in Gloucester, Mass.

Seagulls eating gurry

Loading fish on hand trucks for delivery to factory

THE FLEET IS IN

The fleet is in today! There won't be any headlines in the newspapers or parades through the city, as there are when a fleet of Navy ships comes into port. Fleets of fishing boats arrive and leave almost every day. Their comings and goings are part of the regular job of bringing food to the city.

But fishermen, like sailors in the Navy, brave stormy seas during all seasons of the year. Sometimes they are away for a few days, sometimes for a week or two. The fleet we are watching today has been out for eight days. No cheering crowds are standing on the pier as the boats come gliding in, one after the other. But, even so, many people are eagerly waiting for the fleet: the fishermen's families, the fish auctioneers, the ship owners, the owners of the fish markets, and the pier workers.

Diesel-engined dragger

Schooner, showing dories over forecastle

Fishing boats used to be called *smacks, sloops,* or *schooners.* Why have the names changed? Because the boats themselves are different. In the old days, all fishing vessels were sailboats, whether they were smacks and sloops (with one sail) or schooners with several. Both the big schooners and the smaller sloops could travel only with the help of the wind. But the days of the schooner are gone. Today fishermen don't depend on the wind; all their ships have engines—either steam or Diesel. In the one the power comes from expanding steam; in the other from burning a special oil called Diesel fuel. This is why their trips are safer and faster, and their runs are much shorter. These speedy modern vessels get as many or more fish in much less time than the old sailboats. They have to, because they are expensive to build. The faster they can make the trip to and from the fishing grounds, the more fish, and money, they bring in during the year.

So many boats! At first they all look alike to us, but then we begin to see differences. Some are short, compact, and tub-like; others are as long as 100 feet. On these larger vessels, flat-bottomed rowboats, called dories, are fastened to the decks, usually over the forecastle. We'll find out later how they are used.

Fishermen are friendly people. Even though they are tired from their long trip, they still like to tell you about their work at sea and their life on board. Here's a boat that has just pulled into a slip; it is being tied to the pier by stout ropes. The name, *Nancy Lee*, is painted on the bow or front of the vessel. Next to it is the *Gertrude M.* and next to that the *Evelyn S.* Fishing boats are usually named after women—often the captain's wife or daughter—like many other vessels such as yachts or tugboats.

Of course, we want to go on board. We want to see what the inside of a fishing vessel is like. And we want to hear the fishermen's stories.

"GLAD TO HAVE YOU ABOARD"

We step right off the pier onto the deck of the *Nancy Lee.* Watch out for the long step down, because the deck is not quite level with the floor of the pier. We have lots of questions about all the things we see, but the fisherman doesn't even wait until we ask him.

Right away he shows us his fishing *gear.* Gear is everything that is carried on board for fishing and running the ship. There are nets and lines; anchors and buoys; stacked baskets for bait and other things; thick ropes coiled on posts; and a round drum wound with heavy wire rope like a spool of thread. The fisherman calls it a *winch*. Here we see several metal barrels and over there a number of poles, thick and thin, tall and short. The poles are *rigs*, says the fisherman.

Winch raising metal basket filled with oysters

What are all these things for? The nets and the lines, of course, are used to catch the fish. Some boats use nets and lines only near the bottom of the ocean. If they lower their nets and lines near the bottom of the ocean, they are called *trawlers*. Trawlers go out for *ground fish* like cod, haddock, and flounder, which live near the bottom of the ocean. Boats with nets that skim the ocean, even if the lower end of the net is 100 feet down, are *seiners* (page 12). They bring in fish like mackerel and herring that live near the top of the ocean. Some boats use no nets at all. These, the fishermen tell us, hunt for

Lowering the trawler by cable

swordfish. Swordfishing is much like whale hunting: the fish are harpooned by men who used to go after them in dories, getting really close to their prey. Today they are taken from a platform mounted on the bow (front end of the boat). The harpoon, a long, sharp spear, is used to stab the fish, which is allowed to run until tired. Then it is hauled in with a line attached to the harpoon at one end and to a buoy at the other.

Some boats use only lines. Where there are lines, there are hooks. The stacked baskets hold bait, lines, and hooks. Several lines are cast over the side at the same time, unwinding from the baskets as they sink. In fisherman's language this is *paying out* the line.

The heavy steel-wire rope on the posts and winches

Preparing to harpoon the
swordfish

is called *warp*. It is used for hauling in the nets and for
towing the dories. *Hawsers*—even heavier rope than the
warp—are used to tie the stern, or back of the vessel, to
the pier. The fisherman shows you that the rope is wound
from left to right the way the hands of a clock move, or,
as he says, "like the sun." Every member of the crew
knows ropes are *always* wound this way. If a rope needs
to be unwound in a hurry—in a storm, for instance—it is
important to know that it has been *spooled* the right way.

Those large metal barrels carry gasoline or Diesel fuel. Does this small boat need so much fuel? Yes, says the fisherman, it takes lots of power to buck the waves and tow dories, to say nothing of pulling against the drag of a net bulging with thousands of fish.

And what a job it is to haul up the fish—tons of them! At last we find out what the winches are for. Turn the winch handle one way and it lowers the nets; turn it the other way, and up come the nets heavy with the catch. It takes a lot of hauling power to drag them over the gunwales (pronounced "gunnels"), the railings on a ship, and onto the deck.

When fishing boats were sailboats, the rigs were used to hold the sails. Now rigs have a different use. All kinds of hauling gear is attached to them. A rig is to a boat what a derrick is to land-digging machines.

Those kegs are *buoys*. They are fastened to the edges of the net. Since they are empty, they float and help to spread the net. They are also easy to see from the boat, so the fishermen can know where the net is.

The anchors we see are lowered into water to keep the boat from drifting when the boat is stopped.

All this is gear—the fisherman's tools for bringing in the fish.

"HOME" FOR THE FISHERMAN

Fishermen don't come home every night after work. When the boats are out on a run, the men may be away for two weeks. Then they come back on shore to their

Pulling ropes to untie the cod end of the trawl, to let the fish out

Buoys fastened to edge of net to help spread it, and to locate it in the water

families for a few days—just time enough to "set" (that is for a short stop and rest)—and off they go again. So the boat is where they live most of the time.

The fisherman on the *Nancy Lee* shows us around his "home."

The little house on the foredeck up front is the "fo'c's'le." And no fisherman ever pronounces it *fore-castle*, which is the way the word is really spelled. Behind it is the pilot house, which is the captain's quarters. The captain is also called "skipper" and he is in full command. The crew obeys his orders in all matters of managing the vessel, such as the course to steer in rough seas or to find the best fishing. On very small boats, captain and crew share the fo'c's'le; it is their home at sea. But on the *Nancy Lee* the crew's living quarters are *below* deck (or downstairs, as we would say on shore).

The skipper invites us to see them, and we go down the companionway, stairs so steep that we have to jump to reach the bottom. Here the crew sleeps. This is no fancy

Forecastle, masts, and rigs, with seagulls following the boat

bedroom; it is not even a dormitory. There are only two double-deckers for the crew of eight men. We can barely squeeze in between the narrow hard shelves. Clothes are stowed in a bed-bag under the bunk.

A double-decker in your bedroom is lots of fun, but to a fisherman it is just a bunk—a place to lay his head between *watches*. He usually sleeps only four hours at a time. Then he takes his turn on watch for four hours, while another member of the crew snatches his sleep in the same bunk.

Four hours' work, four hours' rest, then back to work again. The watches are the turns the crew members take at working. At every moment of the day or night some of the men must be on watch, because at sea there is always work to be done: watching for other ships, watching for signs of fish, watching the engine and keeping it going. When the fish are running, the whole crew may work all day and all night without sleeping. When there is a large crew and when things are quiet (when the ship is returning to port, for instance), watches may be 6 hours or even 8 hours long. In between watches the men can sleep.

You can see why the whole crew of a fishing boat never eats together. First one-half of the crew sits down to a meal, then the other half. And they are all hungry! Their sleeping quarters may be cramped and not very comfortable, but the food always tastes good to the hard-working men.

Crew's quarters

When they smell fresh-cooked cod, and the cook calls, they are more than ready to dip into the food on their tin plates. They have fresh-baked bread, fried potatoes, and plenty of strong, hot coffee. With the fish catch and the food the boat carries from shore, fishermen always have plenty to eat.

When fishing is good, the men work around the clock, with no time out for rest. Then, after each catch, there's time for a puff at the pipe, a mug of hot coffee, a game of checkers, or perhaps just for petting the ship's cat. There are always good "fish stories" to tell. Some are just made-up stories, but most are true tales of men lost in dories, of iced up ships, of fogs. The men never tire of telling each other how brave fishermen have met the dangers that come with their special way of making a living.

Gloucester fishermen have a favorite true story of the man who, in an ice storm felt his hands freezing up and bent them around the oars of his dory, before they could become stiff, so that he could continue to row even though his hands were frozen. Then there is the legend of the boat that returned safely with its catch, and not a single one of its crew was there. How they had disappeared, no one ever knew.

WHAT A CATCH!

Our fisherman friend now invites us to see his precious cargo: the fish brought in on the run. They are kept in the *hold*, all the space below decks not used as crew's quarters. It looks like a huge bin, stacked high with thousands and thousands of fish. The fisherman can only guess their weight, but the dock workers will weigh the catch as it is unloaded, and then each fisherman will know how much was caught, and how much he will be paid for his share.

The smaller fishing boats are owned by one, two, or three men who take their share of the catch. The large modern fishing boats are usually owned by a company which hires fishermen who bring in the catch for the company which pays them a wage.

Most fishermen are not paid wages or salaries like men who work in factories or offices. Instead each member of the crew owns a *share* in the catch. Let's say that ten men go out on a boat which brings in 20,000 pounds of fish which sells at $2000. First the owner of the boat gets his share for the expense of maintaining the boat in good repair. Then each crew member receives one-tenth of the rest after the food, ice, and fuel are paid for. When the fishing is good, the fishermen prosper—even if they don't get rich. But when the fish are few and the runs are long, then hard times come to the fisherman and his family.

The *Nancy Lee* is one of the smaller boats you see tied on the wharf. The skipper guesses that the catch in the hold of the *Nancy Lee* is about 20,000 pounds, a very good week's haul for a small boat and its crew. He won't know exactly how big it is until the fish are separated from the ice and weighed.

About ten years ago, the Fish and Wildlife Service,

a government bureau, counted the number of pounds of fish caught in different ways (by nets, lines, etc.) by American commercial fishermen. *Commercial* fishermen are those who earn their living by fishing for large quantities of fish to be sold. Fishermen like you or your father, or your friends who fish just for the fun of it, are called sport fishermen.

The Service also counted the number of fishermen who shared in the total American catch, and how much fish reached American restaurants and dinner tables, by way of fish stores, or wholesale fish dealers.

Here is what the government found out:

Cleaning haddock on board ship

4,400,000,000 pounds of fish were caught in one year;

82,000 fishermen brought in this catch;

Each fisherman caught 53,800 pounds of fish that year;

Almost three-fourths of the total were caught with various kinds of giant nets, the rest with lines or other gear;

1,500,000,000 pounds—about one-third of the haul— ended up as canned fish.

A little more than one-third didn't get to market as fish at all; some was made into *fish meal* (food for chickens and other farm animals), some into oil.

680,000,000 pounds of fresh fish were sold.

The rest was filleted (pronounced "fillayed"), frozen and packaged, cured in barrels, or frozen whole.

AN ICY BED

Catching the fish is only part of the fisherman's job. As soon as the nets are pulled over the side of the boat, he has other work to do. His job on each net full of fish isn't done until the load is safely stored away on ice in the hold. Between loads and before icing, some kinds of fish like cod and haddock are cleaned. The gills are cut out, often the heads are cut off, the fish are slashed down the center and cleaned, the waste is thrown overboard. Cleaning the insides is called *gutting*. Other fish like flounder and hake are not gutted on board; the live fish are lowered onto the bed of ice in the hold.

See the fish lying there between layers of ice chunks. Only in this way can the fisherman bring in his cargo fresh and unspoiled. Ice is as necessary to a fishing boat as fuel and nets.

YOU NAME THE FISH

What kind of fish has the *Nancy Lee* brought? Are you surprised that they are all the same kind—rosefish? Their bright red color gives them their name. (The captain tells you that in Gloucester they are called "redfish" or "ocean perch"). Here and there you may see a small flounder or a whiting, but it seems out of place and in the wrong company. On the pier these strays will be

Ice removed from the hold, where it kept the fish fresh

Rosefish

taken out as waste before the rest of the catch is weighed, for today the pier is marketing only redfish.

Fish, like many other living things, have their own breeding grounds, living and traveling in groups of the same kind. Fishermen know where they will find one or another kind.

All the boats today are bringing the same fish from the same fishing grounds. On other days the catch may be haddock, flounder, or mackerel.

NOT FOR FUN

Commercial fishermen are not fishing for fun. They are toilers of the sea, just as farmers are toilers of the land. To gather the harvest of the sea, seeds do not have to be planted, and the growing crops do not have to be cultivated. But reaping this water "crop" is not one bit easier than harvesting grain, and a great deal more dangerous than working the soil.

Year in and year out, summer and winter, in all kinds of weather, fishermen venture out to bring in the ocean's crop. In raging waters as well as calm seas, they cast their lines and spread their nets. Sometimes their catch is heavy, the nets are bursting full. At other times the fish are few, the nets are "holed" with shark bites, or the

Snow-covered fishing boat arriving in port

trip back is delayed by wind, fog, and storm. And sometimes the ship, with all its crew, never returns at all. The fisherman's work is hard, and the dangers of his life are many.

Most of the fish we eat are caught by large crews on big motor-run boats, equipped with modern gear and ways of keeping the fish fresh for the entire run. Their trawling nets stretch over acres of ocean floor, and their lines reach hundreds of feet below the surface of the water. Their catch is counted not by the number of fish caught, not even in pounds, but in thousands of tons! And each member of the crew can count his yearly haul in tens of thousands of pounds.

CHAPTER TWO

Brave Men

FAR AWAY AND LONG AGO

No one knows who the first fisherman was, because he must have lived thousands of years before histories were written. Long before people grew food by planting seeds in the ground, they had found it in the water. Before they hunted animals in the forest, they hunted fish— picked them up at the edges of drying streams or on land that had been swept by floods.

The first food fish were probably caught with bare hands, for there was no fishing gear that long ago. The fisherman of those ancient days either snatched the fish quickly with his fingers or "tickled" them. In order not to frighten the fish, he would hold his hand motionless in the water, and when a fish swam lazily over it, he tickled its belly. While the fish was enjoying the tickling, the man closed his hand and grabbed the fish from its watery home. Fish are still caught by tickling—trout, for instance, where they glide quietly through calm pools.

Then people learned how to make tools to help them fish. First came spears, then bows and arrows. They harpooned and shot fish in the same way they killed land animals. Harpoons and arrows are still used for fishing today.

About 4000 years ago, the Egyptians began to use fishing poles and lines. Their poles were green sticks, and the lines were braided of animal hair. Instead of hooks, they used sticky burrs. The first real hooks were made of bone. Then came hooks of bronze, and later iron. Nowadays we use steel fish hooks.

With a hook and line even the best fisherman could catch only a few at a time—one to each hook. But a fish net could bring in many at once. Who were the first people to make fishing nets? Perhaps primitive people learned how; we don't know definitely. But in history books we find that the Jews in the Near East discovered how to weave fish nets. After that, fishermen could catch more than enough fish for their own food, and they began to sell the extra catch to other people. Commercial fishing was on its way.

FISH—AND THE PILGRIMS

Did you know that fishing had a lot to do with the founding of the first English colony in North America? Of course, the Indians had fished lakes and streams throughout the length and breadth of the continent for centuries. But even before Columbus' voyage in 1492, Europeans, too, knew that the East Coast of America was a good fishing ground. Stories are told that the Norsemen, among them Eric the Red, sailed all the way to these shores in search of fish. Some people doubt that these stories are true, because it is hard to believe that the Vikings could have made the long, dangerous journey from far away Scandinavia in such tiny boats.

Maybe the Vikings never did reach American shores. But it is true that many, many years before the American colonies were founded, Europeans were fishing off southern Canada. In 1497, the English explorer, John Cabot, reported to King Henry VII that there were plenty of cod near Newfoundland. From then on, European fishermen sailed to American shores and took back ships full of cod to Spain, Portugal, France, and England.

When fishing in these waters became a serious business, fishermen needed land stations—ports where they could get ready for their runs. Without going back to Europe to load up with food and ice, mend their nets and sails, they could prepare for the next trip to the fishing grounds on the American coast. The need for such land stations, and the large number of cod off the coast were two reasons why the first permanent American colony was established in New England.

THE SACRED COD

In 1623, three years after the Pilgrims landed in Plymouth, a company of men arrived from Dorchester,

The golden "Sacred Cod" which hangs in the House of Representatives in Boston

England. With their leader, the Reverend John White, they found a good harbor and they set up their fishing stages, or land stations. This was the beginning of the great fishing port of Gloucester (pronounced *Gloster*) and also of the Massachusetts Bay Colony.

The very first year, this pioneering group of men shipped a cargo of fish to Spain. With this, codfishing as an industry was established in Gloucester. For over three hundred years this city has been a fishing port. It is the oldest in the United States and still one of the largest in the world.

Codfishing as an industry brought so much wealth to New England that the ship owners, ship builders, and fish merchants were called the "codfish aristocracy." The cod was called the "sacred" fish.

Most state capitol buildings have pictures of famous pioneers and leaders on their walls. But Massachusetts has a codfish made of gold which originally hung in the Old State House in Boston. In 1798, it was moved to the House of Representatives in the New State House, and on May 6, 1895 was moved again to the new House Chambers, where it may now be seen. This image of the "Sacred Cod" shows how important codfishing was and still is in the life of the people of Massachusetts.

WILL MY SHIP COME IN?

The members of the "codfish aristocracy" in Massachusetts and other New England states traded in fish, but they were not the fishermen. They stayed on shore and waited for their ships to return from long and risky journeys at sea.

"When my ship comes in" is an old expression. It means "when my dreams come true," or "when all is well with me." This saying goes back to the time when the first large ships sailed away to distant countries and came back loaded with goods. Sometimes the ships did not come back and everything was lost. When they did return, the merchants and ship owners had lots to sell, and grew rich.

The codfish merchants of New England waited first for their ships to come in from the fishing grounds. Then they waited for cargoes of exchange goods, such as cloth, spices, salt, rope, and netting to arrive from the European ports, where most of the catch, after being dried and salted, was taken and sold. When the seas were calm, fishing was good and the voyage to and from Europe safe. Their "ships came in," and the merchants made lots of money.

"Will my ship come in?" meant something different

The "Widow's Walk" porch at the top of a house in Gloucester, Mass.

to the fishermen who "went down to the sea in ships."
For them, fishing was often a struggle against ice, snow,
and sleet, fierce gales and blinding fogs, collisions,
pirates, a rockbound coast, and attacks by warring vessels. To their wives and children, the safe return from
the sea meant a happy homecoming and enough food
until the next trip out and the next safe return. If the
ship sank or was wrecked, the merchant lost his fortune,
but the fishermen lost their lives, the wives their hus-
bands, and the children their fathers. And this happened
so often that the little porch you can see on the tops of
many homes on Cape Cod, where the wife watched for
the ship, is called the "Widow's Walk."

THE GLOUCESTER FISHERMAN

The members of the Massachusetts State Assembly
chose to honor the cod, but the people of Gloucester pay

their tribute to the fishermen who died trying to bring
in the fish. They still tell about the terrible storm of 1776
when nine schooners and 40 Gloucester fishermen lost
their lives. They can count nearly 1000 vessels and almost
5000 fishermen who never returned from trips made
between the years 1830 and 1951. Even today, old-timers
remember the men about whom the English author, Rudyard Kipling, wrote his exciting story *Captains Courageous.*

In 1923, 300 years after the city was founded, the
people of Gloucester decided to honor the courage and
bravery of the men who earn their living from fishing in
the open ocean. On August 28th, at the 300th Anniver-
sary Celebration, they unveiled a bronze statue of a fisherman at the wheel of a schooner, steering his vessel

**Recreation room at Fishermen's Institute, Gloucester, where Rudyard
Kipling wrote most of** Captains Courageous

Front view of statue of
Gloucester fisherman

through the perilous sea. When you visit Gloucester,
almost the first thing you see is the statue of the
"Gloucester Fisherman" with his face turned toward the
harbor.

The sculptor chosen to design this statue was Leonard
Craske. The Master Mariners, an association of elder
fishermen, rejected his first model because, they said, it
looked more like a yachtsman than a Gloucester fisherman. They wanted the fisherman dressed in stormy-
weather rig—oilskin coat and fisherman's hat. They
wanted Mr. Craske to go out into the open sea on a fishing schooner, so he could see what life on the fishing
banks was like. And go he did, on the *Elizabeth Noonan*,
and from what he learned made his statue a real, true-to-
life fisherman.

Every year, on a Sunday afternoon in August, the
people of Gloucester gather at this monument to pay
tribute to the fishermen who were lost during that year.

Ceremony in memory of fishermen lost at sea, showing wreaths of flowers on the water

The Roll of Honor of the dead fishermen is read, taps is sounded on a bugle, and hymns are sung. Then the fishermen's children throw wreaths of flowers on the water. As these are carried along with the tide, the love and sad farewells of the fisherfolk go with them out to the sea. And thus the ceremony is ended, until the next year.

Fishermen used to call New England the fishing capital of the nation. The oldest fisheries in the country are in Gloucester, Boston, and New Bedford, Massachusetts, and in Portland, Maine. Today fisheries in other parts of the United States, mainly on the Pacific coast, are larger and more modern. They handle more fish than all the fisheries from Maine to Texas put together.

There are fisheries along the coast of the North,

Middle and South Atlantic states, along the Gulf Coast, on the Great Lakes and the Mississippi River, and along the entire Pacific coast, including Alaska. In the early days in New England the fishermen were English. As our country grew with people from other lands, Portuguese also fished off the same coast; Negro fishermen still take menhaden (relatives of the herring) off the coast of Florida; Italian fishermen work off the coast of Monterey and San Francisco; Mexican and Japanese fishermen on the southern California coast.

CHAPTER THREE

Bringing in the Catch

FISH MAPS

On the next two pages, you will see a fish map of the United States. Now you can see where your favorite fish comes from. It may travel three thousand miles before it reaches your table, or it may come from near-by waters.

Look at the map again. Here are some very important facts for fishermen. Each area has its own particular fish population. Of course, you know that fresh-water fish from lakes and rivers are different from those that live in the salty ocean. But even the sea is not the same everywhere; it may be deep or shallow, warm or cold. Some fish live and breed better in the cool northern waters; others get along best in the warm waters of the south.

Codfish live on sand, rosefish on gravel, the blackback flounder in mud, and haddock on great rocks. Some fish live near the shore; others far out at sea. Fish do not always stay in the same place. Salmon, herring, and shad come inshore at certain seasons of the year.

Fishermen have to know a great deal about the habits of the fish in their area. They have learned just where, when, and how to go after the fish they want. The North Atlantic cod is caught in one way, the Pacific coast salmon in another. Just as the fish are different, so are the ways of fishing.

NORTH, SOUTH, EAST, WEST

These North Atlantic fish, like haddock, cod, rosefish, and flounder, are *ground fish*. They live close to the bottom of the fishing grounds and are caught with *otter trawls*, deep-sea nets like the one in the picture on page 77. The name of these nets comes from the fact that "otter boards" were used by poachers on estates in England to trap otters. The nets are dragged along the ocean floor by large trawlers like the *Nancy Lee*.

Other northern fish, like herring and mackerel, come inshore and to the surface during midsummer and fall, when they lay their eggs. They are usually caught in nets spread out near the surface, or in *weirs*—fenced-in traps set in the quiet waters just beyond the breakers (see picture on page 68).

Most of the catch from New England is shipped fresh or frozen.

In the Middle Atlantic states, oysters, blue crabs, menhaden, shad, and striped bass are fished inshore.

Fish map of the United States

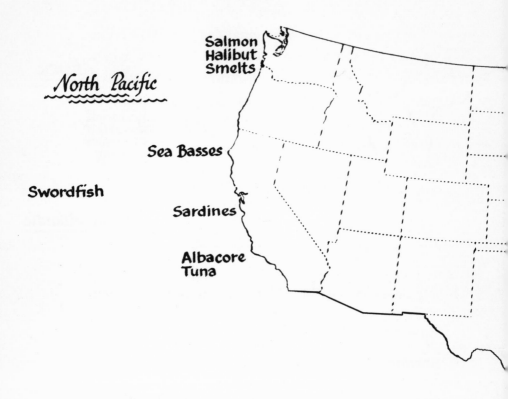

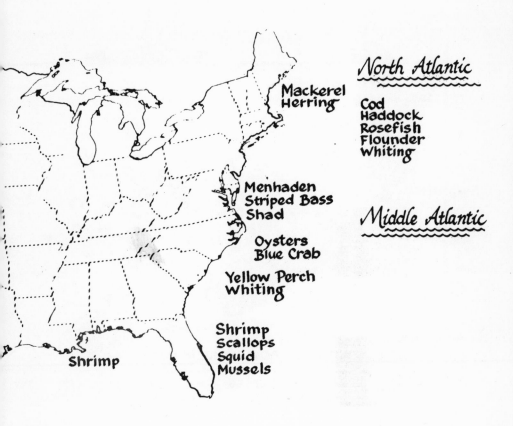

Mackerel
Herring

North Atlantic

Cod
Haddock
Rosefish
Flounder
Whiting

Menhaden
Striped Bass
Shad

Middle Atlantic

Oysters
Blue Crab

Yellow Perch
Whiting

Shrimp
Scallops
Squid
Mussels

Shrimp

The continental shelf and banks

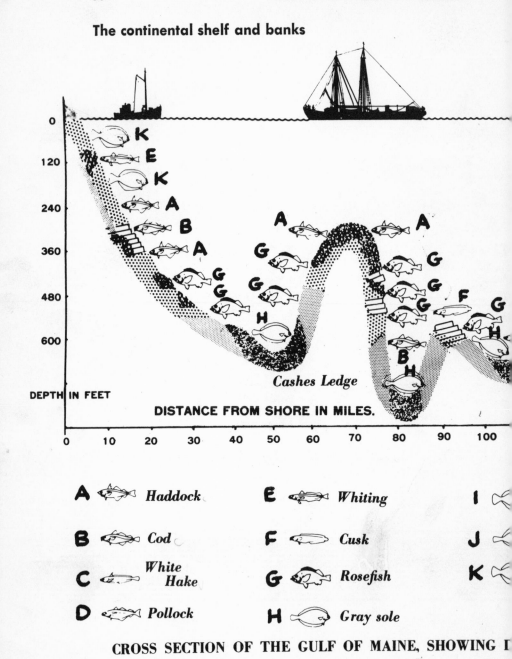

CROSS SECTION OF THE GULF OF MAINE, SHOWING I

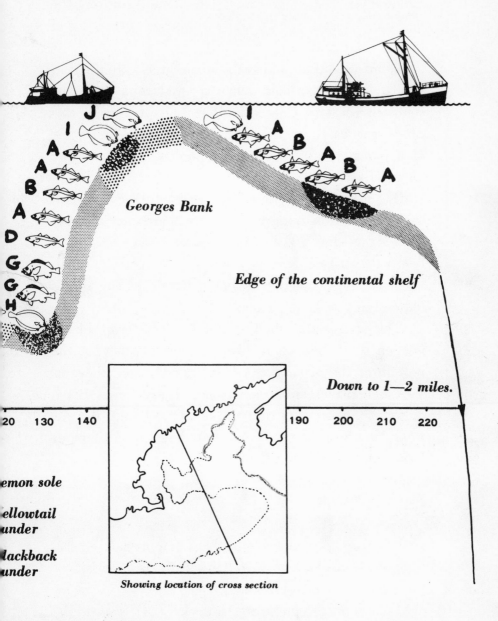

Georges Bank

Edge of the continental shelf

Down to 1—2 miles.

20   130   140   190   200   210   220

emon sole

ellowtail
under

lackback
under

Showing location of cross section

TION OF GROUNDFISH BY DEPTH AND TYPE OF BOTTOM.

While most of the fish from this region are smoked, the crabs are cooked, and the oysters shucked (taken out of their shells) and shipped uncooked.

Salmon, halibut, and crabs come largely from North Pacific shores, sardines, albacore, and tuna from the southern coast of California. The biggest part of this catch reaches your table packed in tin cans, but some of it is made into fish meal for poultry and into other animal feed.

The main fishing grounds are parts of the *continental shelf*. This is an underwater ledge which extends out from shore some 100 to 200 miles. It is about 800 feet below the surface. It ends very suddenly, and the ocean becomes very deep—two or three miles deep. This is also the end of the fishing grounds.

The continental shelf is not flat and level like a kitchen shelf. It is more like a mountain chain at the bottom of the ocean, with hills, valleys, and plateaus. The high places are called *banks*. The Georges Bank, 80 to 220 miles out of Boston, the Grand Banks, Browns Bank, and Seal Island off Newfoundland are all famous fishing grounds.

FISH BIOGRAPHIES

What do you know about the different kinds of fish you eat? Can you recognize them in the fish market, or the window of a restaurant?

Look at the fish pictures. Haddock (p. 54), is one of the most important North Atlantic fish. Its meat is very white

Cod

and firm, and its flavor mild. Haddock is usually filleted (a process we'll find out more about later on). The rest is smoked to make finnan haddie, which you may have eaten in fish chowder. Most of the haddock caught are about a foot and a half long and weigh about three pounds; the largest ever caught in the North Atlantic weighed 37 pounds.

The cod is larger than its relative, the haddock. Notice, in the picture, its large head, short stubby nose, and the wide mouth barbed like a rooster's wattle under its chin. Its skin is spotted, and a long pale line runs from its head to its tail fin. (On the haddock this line is black, which is one way to tell it from the cod.)

The habits of these two fish are different, too. Unlike the haddock, the cod doesn't always stay close to the bottom. Sometimes cod swim close to the surface where fishermen often see them chasing smaller fish. But fishermen have another way of telling where codfish live: by examining the food in their stomachs. Small cod swallow the tiny plants, squid, and herring which live close to the surface. The larger cod live on clams, cockles, mus-

Haddock

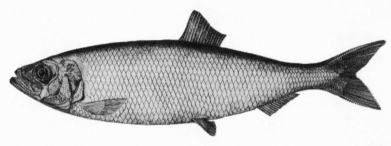

Herring (from drawing by H. L. Todd)

Mackerel (from drawing by H. L. Todd)

sels, starfish, sea cucumbers, and sand worms which they
find closer to the bottom. The codfish swallow these little
animals whole. Their meat is digested in the fish's stom-
ach, and the shells left stacked like a nest of ash trays.

The smallest cod, called *scrod*, weigh about two pounds. The "market cod" weigh up to 10 pounds, and the largest cod weigh over that. Cod as heavy as 50 or 60 pounds are often caught. Sometimes one of these big fellows is displayed in the window of a restaurant where people stop to admire it.

Rosefish (see page 33), the catch we saw on the *Nancy Lee,* is a new discovery of U. S. fisheries. Fishermen have known this pretty orange-red fish for a long time, but people didn't eat much of it until recently. Why has it finally become a popular dinner fish? Here's the story.

There are millions of fish in the ocean, and more millions of young hatch every day. Even so, one kind of fish may become very scarce. Sometimes more fish are caught than are replaced by hatching; or else too many fish are caught before they are old enough to lay eggs. Both of these things happened to haddock.

In 1935, the year the haddock catch was smallest, fishermen remembered the rosefish. Usually they had thrown these fish overboard because only a few got into the nets with thousands of haddock. But now they found that rosefish made good eating, so they went after this brightly colored, smaller fish with its large, spiny head, and dark eyes. Today an occasional haddock or whiting in a rosefish catch gets thrown overboard as waste, just as the rosefish used to be!

In 1930, 118,000 pounds of rosefish were caught, but in 1935 the number jumped to over 17,000,000, and in 1941 it was more than 145,000,000! Rosefish are sold mostly as fillets, either fresh or frozen, and as cooked-and-frozen "fish-sticks" (more about these later). Rosefish live near the bottom, and most of the catch comes from a depth of 300 to 700 feet. They are caught all year round, mainly during the day, when they stay together close to the bottom and can be netted with otter trawls. At night they scatter, with some rising toward the surface. They are then difficult to catch in large numbers.

Rosefish is one of the few food fish whose young hatch from eggs *inside* the mother, instead of from eggs left in the water. The young are born in the summer and grow about an inch each year. They are fully grown after ten years, when they weigh about 1½ pounds.

SCHOOLS OF FISH

Thousands and thousands of fish swimming along at top speed! The water is dark with them. Their strong, streamlined bodies ripple the surface like a wave. This great parade of fish goes on—and on—and on. A school of herring is passing by!

Herring, mackerel, and many other fish that live close to the surface of the water travel in these enormous groups, called *schools*. They are easy to catch with surface nets. Sea herrings are among the earliest fish that people caught in nets. Today the larger herring are smoked and sold as *bloaters* or else salted; but most of the young herring are packed as sardines. The herring that don't reach the dinner table are used for fish meal to feed animals. The scraps end up as oil in paint.

The life of the herring is a risky one. Many do not even live long enough to end up in a fisherman's net; they are eaten by haddock, cod, bluefish, salmon, shark, tuna, or swordfish. Haddock and cod also eat herring eggs, which they find in clusters on rocks and weeds at the bottom of the sea. Even winds and tides are the herring's enemies. Schools of young herring and herring eggs are often washed ashore, where the fish die and the eggs are destroyed. In spite of this, so many herring hatch and grow that millions of pounds are caught. The herring catch brings thousands of dollars to the fishermen and millions to the packers.

Mackerel, too, travel in very large schools, sometimes miles long. They spend their winters at the bottom of the sea and come inshore every spring. They reach Chesapeake and Delaware Bays in April and the New England waters in May and June. The eggs are left in surface waters; and when the young are hatched, they feed on the rich seaweed and tiny animals over the continental shelf.

Mackerel are taken either with large nets that surround a whole school at once, or with small nets left in the water overnight. Fishermen like to use large nets on dark nights, when there is no moon. Then they can see fish more easily, because they are feeding on small sea animals that glow like fireflies. In a spot where the fish are gathered, the ship's lookout sees a blanket of light spread over the ocean. Then the crew surrounds the school with their widely spread net. On moonlit nights, the fishermen can't see the glow of the tiny ocean ani-

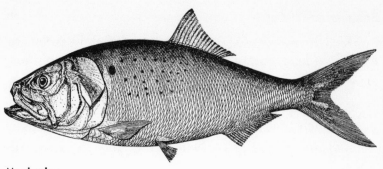

Menhaden

mals, so they lower the smaller nets into the water early in the evening. During the night the fish swim into them, and in the morning the fishermen pull them in.

Mackerel is a very oily fish, and spoils easily. So it is thoroughly iced at sea. When it reaches port, it is immediately sold. If it is not sold fresh right away, it must be salted or smoked for sale later on.

Another fish, the menhaden, is also caught off the Middle Atlantic States, and in Chesapeake Bay. Like its cousin, the herring, it travels in schools and lives near the surface. The young start their lives in the bays, sounds, and large rivers of New England. During the first year they grow to be 6 inches long. The second year they almost double in length, and increase their weight 6 or 7 times! At the age of three to four years, they are fully grown and are very fat and oily. Their oil makes them very valuable to fishermen. Except for their roe, or eggs, they are rarely used as food for people, but as fish meal for animals and for many other purposes you will read about later.

When fully grown, they start their journey from New

England to the warmer ocean waters of the south. On this trip they are captured in nets and fish traps.

WATER HIGHWAYS

Schooling fish are great wanderers. They swim up and down the coast or from the shore out to sea. Often they cover hundreds of miles in a season. Fishermen have gotten to know their watery paths, so they are easily found and caught each season.

These fish migrants, such as mackerel, tuna, herring, and swordfish, travel for two reasons: to look for food and to find places to lay their eggs. They are powerful swimmers, with their long, streamlined bodies that move swiftly through the water.

Another migrating fish is the striped bass. Every

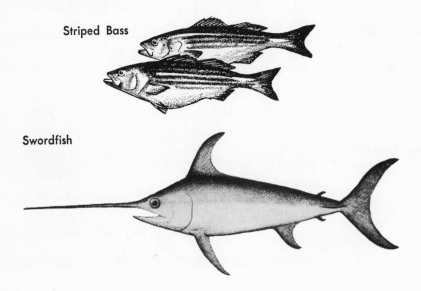

Striped Bass

Swordfish

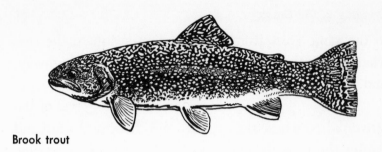

Brook trout

spring they move out from their wintering places in the
bays and rivers that empty into the Middle Atlantic, and
travel north to New England. Every fall they make the
return journey. Some groups may break away from the
main mass of fish and stop at some spot along the way,
but most of them swim back to where they started.

Some fish migrate only once during their whole lives.
When salmon are fully grown and ready to lay eggs, they
begin a long, long journey late in the summer. Far out
in the ocean, they gather in swarms (which are smaller
than schools). They swim toward shore, back to the river
where they were born. They continue swimming up the
river, making their way to the spawning grounds. There
they lay their eggs and then some, like the Pacific salmon,
die after the one spawning. Each salmon always returns

King Salmon

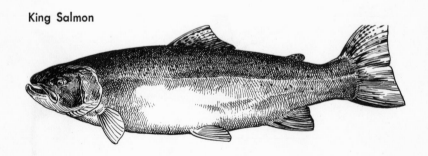

to the same river from which it first swam to the sea. That river is the salmon's birthplace, its watery highway, and its grave.

A male and a female build a nest in the gravel of the stream's bed where the eggs are laid. During the fall and winter the eggs develop and hatch early in the spring. After feeding for two months on what is left of the eggs, the young fish, now called *fry*, work their way out of the

Sea mussel

Bay scallop

Blue crab

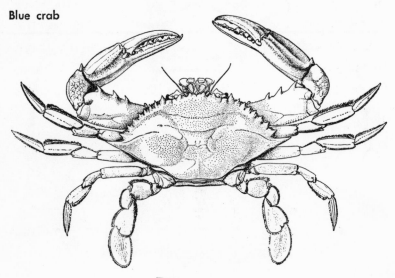

gravel and start looking for food. In their search they
travel down the river highway to the sea, where they
stay until they are old enough to lay eggs of their own.
Then they start back over the same path to the place
from which they came.

Lobster of Florida (rock lobster)

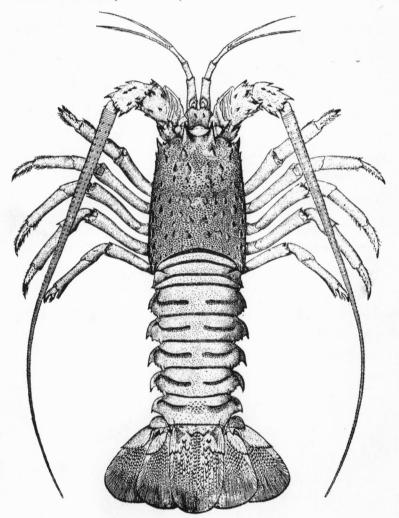

Some fish are stay-at-homes. They move very little, just higher and lower in the water or closer to shore at night. Brook trout hide in quiet pools by day and swim out into the main current during the night only to get food.

Then there are other sea creatures, not really fish at all, which always stay in the same place. Often they are attached to rocks or piers. Among these are lobsters, crabs, oysters, clams, mussels, and scallops, all of which we call "seafood."

These and many other creatures including fish, which people use as food, live in the seas and fresh water. The Department of the Interior of our government in Washington distributes booklets which describe them, and tell about their special habits.

Fishermen are always learning more about the life habits of fish: the kind of food they eat, how they get it, where they lay eggs, how the young grow up, how large and how old they must be to have young. The more fishermen know, the more fish they can catch. By knowing these things, they can also keep from killing off any one kind of fish. More and more, scientists are also helping fishermen to learn more about the ocean and the creatures in it.

CHAPTER FOUR

All Kinds of Gear

HOOK, LINE, AND SINKER

Knowing when and where to find the fish is one part of
the skipper's job. But he also has to know which gear
to use. This depends on the kind of fish he is after and
the waters where they are found. There are many kinds
of fishing gear: hooks and lines, mazes and traps, nets
which encircle, and nets which entangle.

Both the sportsman and the commercial fisherman
use hooks and lines—the oldest gear, but still good for
catching fish. Commercial hook-and-line fishing is of two
kinds: *trolling* for schools of fish on the surface, and
trawling for groundfish.

In trolling, lines are hung over the stern of the vessel
and fastened to outrigger poles on deck. Each line,
weighted with a lead sinker, is run through a small block
to its own reel, so that it can be reeled separately. Then

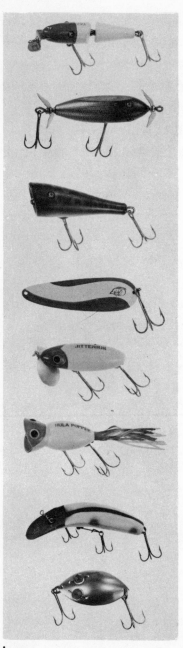

Lures

the lines are towed at just the right speed to keep the hooks near the surface. The heavier the sinker, the deeper the line goes; but the faster the boat moves, the nearer to the surface comes the line. It takes skill and experience to troll at exactly the right depth.

The hooks are usually baited with whole small fish or pieces from the side of a larger one. Sometimes *lures* are used instead of live bait. The lure may be a metal spinner or a little bunch of feathers which attracts the fish. Fishermen like to use lures because they save the cost of bait, and the work of re-baiting the hook between catches. But fish will not always bite at lures, so then live bait has to be used.

Pacific tuna and Florida red snapper are caught with hook and line. So are king mackerel, king salmon, and albacore.

Trawl lines are not towed, but are lowered into the

Line trawl in operation from dory

deep water where bottom-feeding fish live. One very long line, called the *ground line,* is lowered until it lies along the ocean bottom. It is kept in place with anchors. Many short lines are fastened to the ground line. Each ground line is also tied to a *keg float.* These little barrels float on the surface and keep the lines in place. Floats are also made of hollow glass or large pieces of cork. Every short line has its own baited hook. The ground line, made of heavy hemp rope, is about 150 feet long. Tied to it about every three feet are the short lines. So one ground line can carry about 50 short lines with 50 hooks for 50 fish!

Trawl line fishing is mostly done from dories, those small boats nested on the deck of the *Nancy Lee.* Each dory usually carries six baskets like the ones you saw on deck, and each basket has a trawl line coiled inside.

When the vessel reaches the fishing banks, the dories are lowered into the water, and the fishermen row out with their baskets. One after another, the lines are paid out. While the fishermen are setting the gear, the boats move along at half speed. Then, when the end of one line is reached, it can be fastened to the next one, until the whole line is several miles long! At various points the line is buoyed up by additional floats to keep it in place. When the entire line is set, the fishermen row back to the beginning and start to haul it in a little at a time. The fish are taken off the hooks and put into the boat, the lines are rolled up into the tubs.

Trawl lines are still used for haddock fishing on the North Atlantic coast. But line trawling is rapidly being replaced by deep net fishing. Dory fishing, too, is going out of style. You'll find out why when we watch a trawl net at work.

FISH IN TRAPS

Some fish are caught in traps. A fish trap is a one-way road for the fish. It has a small opening where the fish enter easily, but once they are inside, they cannot get back through the opening. A trap may be quite small and easy to carry from place to place, or it may be a tremendous fenced-off area where whole schools of fish are caught at one time. *Weirs* and *pound nets* are two kinds of large traps (see pictures on pages 68 and 70).

In ancient times, people made fish traps out of brush and stones. Long ago, Indians in Alaska built a sort of dam in which they caught salmon as they swam upstream on their way to the spawning grounds. The dam was made in the shape of a funnel. At the small end of the funnel, the fish found themselves in a basket trap from

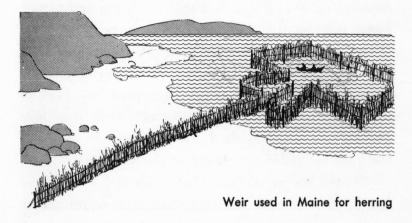

Weir used in Maine for herring

which they could easily be taken. Even today in some small European fishing villages, dams of this type are set in fast-moving streams to trap the fish.

You will find weirs at many places in the streams and coastal waters of New England. In the spring, fishermen

Alewife

set their traps to catch alewives, relatives of the herring. In the late summer and fall, they trap eels as they travel downstream toward the ocean to lay their eggs. At the right season you can see the hickory or bamboo stakes sticking up out of the water. Heavy cotton webbing hangs from these posts. The weir has three parts: a long fence running out from the shore, a small enclosure, and a large enclosure—all made with posts and webbing.

This is how a weir works. As the fish swim along, they are stopped by the fence, which they follow until they reach the opening of the weir. They are now caught in the smaller of the two enclosures. They swim through this one and into the large enclosure, where the webbing has rings all around its lower edge, with a heavy rope

Men in boats lifting pound nets

running through the rings. This pulls the webbing into a giant bag, from which there is no escape for the trapped fish!

Now the trap-boat draws alongside the weir and fishermen dip the fish out with a big dipnet. Hundreds of barrels of fish are sometimes taken from a single weir.

Along the Atlantic coast and the Great Lakes fish are caught in *pound nets* built of wire and cotton netting. These are much larger than weirs, and they are different in other ways. The large enclosure of the trap has walls of webbing like a weir, but it also has a webbed floor, because it is too big to be drawn into a bag. Small stakes are not strong enough to hold it up, so it is kept in place by heavy ropes and anchors.

To build a pound, posts are driven into the bottom where the water is shallow. The posts outline the shape of the pound: two enclosures and a long fence running out from shore like a weir. Next a metal cap is bolted

Pile trap (photo by Paul Thompson)

to the top of each post, and wire mesh netting is fastened to the caps to make the fence and traps. The larger enclosure also has tarred cotton webbing with either fine or wide mesh. A pound net for the small herring, which are later packed as sardines, has small-sized mesh, while a net for catching salmon has much wider openings in the mesh. This kind of pound is called a *pile trap*.

Floating trap

Where the water is too deep or the bottom too rocky for driving posts, a *floating trap* is set. This is made of logs, fastened by wire cables to concrete anchors on the bottom. Three of these anchors, which weigh up to five tons each, hold the trap in place, and the net is hung from the floating log frame.

Like weirs, pound nets are used for catching school fish, such as herring or salmon. The fish meet up with the fence—called the *leader*—and swim along the wire netting. Soon the whole school has passed through the first enclosure, or *heart*. From there they go through a tunnel into the large net-floored chamber, the *pot*.

As the fish swim round and round in the pot, the fishermen come to take them out. A fishing boat, towing a barge, pulls up close to the trap. Then begins the *brailing* of the fish. The brail is a piece of heavy netting which is lowered into the trap. When the fish swim over it, a power machine raises it up and over the side of the barge, full of live fish. Thousands and thousands of trapped fish are carried to shore on the barges.

When the season is over at one spot, the fishermen remove the trap and set it up at another place where they think the fishing will be good.

COME INTO MY PARLOR

Weirs and pound nets are built to catch fast-swimming fish. Small traps, called *pot gear*, are used to catch the slow-moving creatures that live close to shore on sea or lake bottoms. A pot is a box-like trap shaped like either

a cylinder or a half-cylinder, with curved top and flat
bottom. It looks a little like a wood-and-wire cage for
carrying pets on a train or bus. The frame is built of
strips of wood and the open spaces are covered with wire
mesh. A pot is usually about four feet long, two feet wide,
and a foot and a half high. Like the giant traps, a pot has

Lobster pot

two compartments: the place where the fish enters, called the *chamber;* and the one where it is trapped, the *parlor.*

The chamber has two entrances, one at each end of the pot. Once in the chamber, the fish pass through a wire tunnel, which narrows down to a few inches at the entrance to the parlor. In lobster pots the bait is placed in the center of the pot at the end of each tunnel, an invitation to the lobster to come into the parlor.

Pot gear is set out on the ocean bottom, 10 or 15 traps in a row, and anchored down with flat stones, bricks, or concrete. How can the fishermen find them again? The spot is marked by floats of cork or glass, tied to the ropes by which the pots were lowered. Pot gear is used to catch lobsters, crabs, and octopi, as well as catfish, eels, sea bass and tropical fish which live on underwater reefs.

The pots are left alone for a day or more, long enough to trap the lobsters or crabs. Then the fishermen come back in small boats. Each man has floats of a different color, so he can find his own pots. The pots are pulled up, loaded on the boats, and then emptied into wooden tanks moored near the shore. The bottoms and sides of these tanks are made of wooden slats, which allow the sea water to flow in and out. That's why the lobster you buy is still alive to wiggle his claws at you!

Sections of woven eel trap. The strips at the funnel's point let an eel in, but not out.

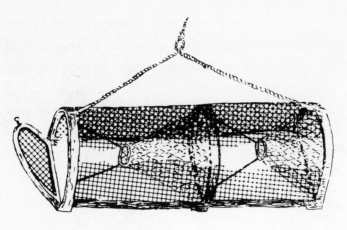

Wire eel trap

Eels are usually caught by professional crab fishermen in the streams along the Middle Atlantic coast. They trap them in an ordinary wire basket. (For a hundred years or more, they used baskets, shaped like a funnel, woven of fine strips of oak.) Nowadays, the eels swim into the wire basket through a funnel made out of a long nylon stocking with the toe cut out. Believe it or not!

CAUGHT IN A PURSE

Not all school fish are trapped; some are surrounded by big, loose nets. A *purse seine* is like a huge ribbon made of fine cotton netting. The upper edge has a string of corks which keep it afloat. The lower edge sinks, because it has a row of lead weights and rings with a rope through them. When the net is lowered into the water, it forms a great wall across the path of the fast-swimming fish.

Fishing vessels which use the purse seines are called

Purse seining

seiners. (These ships were described on page 21.) The captain waits for a school of fish: mackerel, menhaden, herring, tuna, or salmon. When he sights it, the net is lowered right away. Moving at full speed, the boat tows the net right around the school of fish. As soon as the circle is complete and the school surrounded, the rope is drawn together like the strings of a handbag. This closes the bottom of the seine, and the fish are caught inside the giant bag or purse. A power engine pulls up the net, and the fish are brailed out with a dipnet.

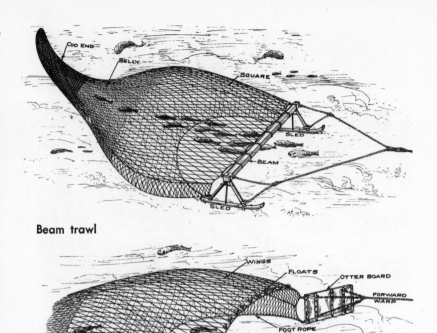

Beam trawl

Otter trawl

Purse seines are about the largest of all single fishing nets; they catch more fish than any other type of net. But they can only be used for fish that swim on the surface.

For groundfish and the fish that live in the depths of the sea, *trawls* are necessary.

DRAGGING THE OCEAN BOTTOM

A trawl is a net made into the shape of a cone, with the wide end open. In the *beam* trawl, this open end is

Gill net at low tide

spread out with a wide board—the beam. The *otter* trawl
has two wings at the open end. Each wing is fastened to
an oak board, with heavy iron strapping. As the net is
dragged, the pressure of the water keeps the mouth wide
open, so that the fish can be scooped up in the net. The
tip end of the trawl, made of fine mesh, is called the
cod end.

Trawlers sail out a long way from shore, to a spot
where the deep promises good fishing. There the net is
paid out with long ground wires, while the boat circles
the net, towing it along at slow speed. When the net is
full, it is hauled on board. First the wires are pulled in
and wound on big drums. Then the net is emptied from
the cod end which is hoisted, the bow knot which ties
it is pulled, and out tumble the fish onto the deck.

Trawls are smaller than purse seines, and they are
lowered much deeper to bring in the groundfish. They

are also taken farther out to sea, out to the Banks. They are the most modern gear for getting bottom fish, which used to be caught from dories. The trawlers or draggers, used in this type of fishing, are strongly built vessels with powerful engines. They can make the trip to the Banks and back at high speed. The fish are cleaned on board and packed in ice. Salt is not necessary any more. Because the trips are so quick, the fish are brought in fresh and all ready to be sold.

TANGLED IN A NET

Gill nets trap the fish in a very different way—in the holes in their cotton mesh. When a fish's head enters the hole, its gills catch in the webbing. It's easy for the fish to get in, but then it's stuck, like a fly in a spiderweb.

The net is hung loosely, with sinkers for weights and corks for floats. Mesh of different size is used for each type of fish. Some are caught around the middle of the body, some around the jaw bone or teeth. As the fish struggles to get away, its gills tangle up in the mesh, so it cannot escape.

Purse seines *surround* the fish, trawls *scoop* them up, gill nets *entangle* them—three important ways of bringing in the catch.

CHAPTER FIVE

The Fish-Pier Market

WHILE THE CITY SLEEPS

You have to get up very early to see what goes on at the fish pier market. Between four and five o'clock in the morning is the busiest time!

The city is asleep. The street lamps are lit, for it is not yet dawn. Everywhere the city is quiet, except on the streets near the fish wharves. Trucks are rolling up; others are parked, waiting. The truckmen and the fish buyers are having their breakfast of coffee and doughnuts in the small restaurants close to the piers. The fishing fleet is just coming in. And while the fish are still on the boats, the catch will go on sale.

HOW MUCH AM I BID?

In the dark hours of the early morning the wholesale fish buyers have gathered together in the auction room

Fish dealers' stalls

on the pier. On one wall is a huge blackboard, where a man is chalking up the names of the boats that are already docked or are just now tying up at the pier.

In one column he writes the name of the boat: the *Nancy Lee,* the *Gertrude M.,* the *Evelyn S.* The next

Dealers and customers

Auction room

column tells what kind of fish the boat has brought in: haddock, cod, or hake, rosefish, or mackerel. Next to this he writes a number: the number of tons each catch weighs. Up to now, the buyers have been just standing around talking fish. Now they all turn toward the blackboard. The auctioneer is standing on the platform, ready to begin.

He reads off the first line on the blackboard. The first boatload is up for sale! Who will make the first bid? Then a buyer shouts his bid: "Five cents!" He is offering to buy the entire boatload of 18,000 pounds for five cents a pound. (In some auctions the bids are made on a thousand pounds—$50 instead of 5 cents.) The auctioneer repeats the bid: "I'm offered five, I'm offered five, who will raise it?" Another buyer calls, "Six cents," still another cries "Seven," and a third, "Nine cents." The auctioneer repeats the new bid, "I'm offered nine, nine, who will give ten, who will give ten?" The first buyer offers ten, while the second bidder says nothing. Again the auctioneer: "I've been offered ten, ten, ten, who will offer eleven, who offers eleven? Going at ten, going at ten, gone at . . . ." And he strikes his hammer on the counter. The first bidder has the boatload: 18,000 pounds at 10 cents a pound. He has bought it for $1,800. The board man crosses out the first line on the blackboard. The buyers look at the next line and get ready to bid. And so the auction goes on until every boat's catch has been sold.

An hour or so later, when the sale is over, the buyers add up their bills for the fish they have bought, and pay them at the cashier's window opposite the board. Some buyers have not bought at all that day; others have bought two loads or more. Now the auction room empties, but the buyers will be back another day to bid on other catches.

Many fish are not brought to auction at all. These are the catch brought in on "company boats" belonging to fish-processing companies. But all the fish is delivered to the dock, where other workers quickly get busy.

DE-ICING AND WASHING

Remember that the fish on the *Nancy Lee* were packed in ice. Before anything can be done to the catch —before it is weighed even—the fish and ice must be separated. That wire cage on the dock is an ice sifter.

De-icer. Ice falls out through holes

About eight feet long and three feet across, it rests on a machine that keeps it going round and round. It has holes large enough for the chunks of crushed ice to fall through, but too small for the fish. The workmen empty large canvas buckets of fish and ice into the cage, and as it moves around, the ice drops through the openings.

Fish being washed on escalator

Now the de-iced fish are ready to start on their trip to the inside of the pier building. Let's follow them.

To keep the fish from being damaged, the inside of the metal sifter is very smooth. So is the metal chute on which the fish leave the sifter. The chute looks very much like a slide in a playground. But this is a moving slide, for it travels along a motor-driven conveyor belt, with its load of fish. First it moves through an opening in the side of the pier building. Once inside, the belt carries the slide slowly through a bin where the fish are washed. Water is squirted on them from sprinklers. Still on the chute, they leave the bin on their way to the scaler.

THE FISH GETS A SHAVE

Have you ever seen fish scaled in your local market? The man pulls the scales off one fish at a time with a sharp scraper that he slides under them. He holds the fish firmly by the head with one hand, while he works the scraper with the other, moving it from tail to head. Even a fast worker cannot scale many fish this way. A

Hand electric shaver (left). Descaling machine (middle). Scales dropping out of machine at bottom; scaled fish go into the box in front of machine (right).

few fish are scaled by hand on the fish pier, too. These are the ones sold right on the dock to fill small orders. But here we find hand-scaling with a difference. The workers use electric scalers, which look and sing just like electric razors. They "shave" the fish at high speed. Z-z-zip, z-z-zoo, the scales are off! The workers dip the fish into ice water to clean away any loose scales, and that's all there is to it.

But when thousands and thousands of fish have to be scaled in a hurry, even this quick way of shaving one fish at a time is much too slow. A scaling machine, powered by electricity, does the job—and much faster. When the fish reach the scaling machines they are taken out of the chute and placed head first on a moving belt. As they are carried through the machine, a number of electric "razors" go to work on them until they have no scales left.

Now the smooth fish leave the machine and travel on another moving belt to the work tables.

WHICH FISH IS FRESH?

Years ago housewives bought most of their fish "in

Steps in hand filleting
Removing head
Breaking backbone
Cutting to remove dorsal fin
Removing fin

the round"—with all the scales on and uncleaned. Why did they go to all the trouble of scaling and cleaning the fish themselves? Because they wanted to be sure the fish was fresh, and they could tell this only when the fish was whole. Seeing the whole fish they could tell if the eyes were bright, clear, and firm—neither bulging nor sunken; if the gills were pink and free from slime. They could smell the gills and know that the fish was fresh. They could see whether the scales were tight and shiny, or loose and dull. And of course, they would always press the fish's body to see if the flesh was firm.

People still like to test the fish they buy "in the round." But today, very few people buy fish that way— it is no longer necessary. Nowadays fish are well cared for, properly stored and preserved, so the housewife can save herself work by giving the fish factories the job of examining, scaling, and cleaning the fish.

FILLET MEANS "NO BONES"

Now the scaled fish is ready for dressing or cleaning. Most of this work is still done by hand. The workers are

lined up on opposite sides of a long cutting table, and the moving belt brings them the fish from the scaling machine. With one quick motion they cut the entire length of the belly and take out the insides. Watch their hands fly, as they cut off the fins, tail, head and upper fins.

The next step is filleting. The word *fillet* can mean a lot of things, such as a strip of cloth or a hair-ribbon. But these meanings have nothing to do with fish! A fish fillet is a strip of boneless meat cut from the fleshy parts of the sides of the fish. With one stroke of a sharp knife from tail to head, the worker slices the flesh away from the backbone in one piece. Then he turns the fish over and does the same thing to the flesh on the other side.

Now watch the fillet being skinned. It is laid flat on the cutting table, skin side down. The worker holds the tail end with his fingers, and skillfully cuts the flesh from the skin. Two fillets from one fish are ready for packing.

You can see that even with a sharp knife and a pair of very skilled hands, this way of filleting takes time, since the fish are cut up one by one. That is why filleted fish costs more per pound than the whole fish. Of course,

Automatic filleting

you can eat every scrap of a pound of fillet—you aren't paying for heads, tail, insides, bones, and skin that you have to throw away.

If scaling can be done by machine, why not filleting? As a matter of fact, some fisheries do have filleting machines with moving belts like the scalers. The earliest filleting machine could be used only on cod and haddock, but improvements were made until now a modern machine can slice fillets from fish weighing only half a

Steps in hand filleting

Cutting fillet from tail to head
Cutting along backbone to remove fillets
Freeing fillet at the tail
Removing skin from fillet

pound. A filleting machine is very complicated and very expensive, so not all fisheries have them. It takes care of all different sizes of fish, frees the flesh from the bone, and takes off the fins and the skin.

One machine can cut fillets from 15,000 pounds of fish in one day. One man operates the part of the machine that cuts off the head, while another feeds the headless fish into the filleting part. The job is done quickly; and the fish are freer from the bacteria which they pick up from the wooden cutting tables.

DRESSED UP IN CELLOPHANE

The fillets are now ready for packing. They continue their ride on the moving belt to still another table, where they are wrapped. This is done by hand, and most of the workers are women. Each worker weighs the fillets on a small scale and wraps them up in one-pound, two-pound, five- or ten-pound packages. Today they are working on one-pound packages. Tomorrow they may work only on larger ones—ten-pound packages. It saves time to pack one size at a time.

An open cardboard box is set on the scale. Clear paper that looks like cellophane lines the box, and the fillets are placed in this wrapping. Enough fish is put in to balance the scale at just the right weight, plus the weight of the wrappings. The label on a one-pound box reads "16 ounces net weight." *Net* weight is the weight of the fish without the box and paper.

Next the box is closed, and the belt takes it over to a

machine which seals up the paper at one end. The package is now ready to be put on racks and sent to the freezing plant. It will arrive in the stores as frozen fish.

Only part of the catch will go to the freezing plant. The rest will be packed for sale right away as fresh fish.

A QUICK TRIP

Many fresh fillets are packed in tin boxes, holding five or ten pounds and lined with the kind of paper that was used in the other packages. The fillets are placed in layers inside the box, and covered with more paper. Then on goes the lid, and off go the boxes on a refrigerated truck to the fish market. Cold, but not frozen, the fillets reach the end of their trip fresh and ready to cook.

On the menus of many restaurants you can read in large letters: "The fish that slept in the ocean last night

Packaging fillets   **Fillets packed in tin boxes**

rests on your plate today." And indeed the whole trip from pier to plate takes only a few hours.

BARRELS OF LEFT-OVERS

How many parts of the fish never get into a cardboard package or a tin box! As it was cleaned and dressed, the fish lost its scales, head, fins, backbone, skin, and insides. Only the fleshy white fillet was left. What happens to all the rest: more than half of the fish when it was in the round? The foreman of the fish factory will tell you that hardly a scrap is wasted.

True, a small part of the waste—heads, guts, skin, and bones—is dumped back into the sea. This is the *gurry* we saw out on the pier. The sea gulls around the pier gobble up a lot of it, and the rest finds its way into the bellies of other fish.

What else happens to the "waste" parts of the fish? We'll find out more about that later. Now let's see how fish can be kept not for just a few hours, but for years!

CHAPTER SIX

How to Keep a Fish

THE LEFT-OVER CATCH

Have you ever caught a fish on a camping trip and cooked it for breakfast over an open fire? M-m-m-m, there's nothing in the world that tastes so good! Fish probably tasted just as good to people long ago, when that was the only way they knew of preparing it. But, suppose the fishing was especially good, and people caught more than they could eat at one meal? All the leftover fish had to be thrown away because they didn't know how to preserve it.

It took hundreds of years for people to find out how to save the extra catch. They also found that preserving fish made it taste different. The first method of preserving fish was *curing*. The fish were dried, smoked, salted, or pickled in vinegar and spices. Often two or more kinds of curing were, and still are, combined to give a new taste.

FISH IN A FACTORY

Believe it or not, less than one-tenth of the fish caught in the United States is sold in local fish markets and eaten fresh. All the rest is preserved so that it can be eaten long after it is caught. How many ways of preserving fish can you count? How many kinds of preserved fish turn up on your dinner table? Today we can buy fish canned, dried, smoked, pickled, or frozen. And that's not all: we can buy dried fish in flakes, canned fish in chowders, frozen fish already fried in deep fat or made into pies. You can probably think of still other kinds of preserved fish. In all these forms, the fish reaches your table months or even years after it was caught—but still perfectly good to eat.

The work of preserving fish is done in fisheries like

Salmon drying on racks in Alaska (photo by C. F. Townsend)

the one you are visiting. We can really call them fish factories. They are found in fishing centers, like Gloucester and New Bedford, Nova Scotia and Alaska, San Francisco and Seattle, New Orleans and Baltimore. Fish from these factories travel thousands of miles. You can eat Pacific salmon in New York or Florida swordfish in Oregon. Even if you live far from any sea or lake, you can still get just about any kind of fish you want.

HANGING UP TO DRY

Food spoils when bacteria get to it before we do. When too many bacteria grow on our food, they make it unfit to eat. But bacteria need heat and moisture to stay alive. We can stop them from growing on our food by keeping it either very cold or very dry. People in ancient

Cod drying in Gloucester, Mass.

times didn't know about bacteria, but they did know that a dried fish could be eaten long after it was caught.

Drying and smoking are almost as old as the discovery of fire, and they are still used today. They are inexpensive methods, because they require none of the expensive equipment used in more modern methods. The first way of preserving fish was by natural air-drying. In the Stone Age, when people were still using stone tools, they learned to dry their extra food to keep it from spoiling.

Fish are still preserved by air-drying in many places like India, China, Japan and the Philippines, where the weather is warm and dry and there are steady winds. Simple air-drying is very much like drying clothes on a clothesline but it takes a little longer—from one to two weeks.

Salmon are split all the way down the middle, except for the small part close to the tail. Then they are hung flesh side out, over wooden "lines" suspended from crossed poles. The uncut tails hold the fish in place like clothespins. Halibut and large flounders are cut into strips before drying. Sometimes they are hung on the rigging of fishing vessels to dry. When the boats reach port after a good run, they look like moving fish racks.

All dried fish is usually soaked for a few hours before it is cooked. Then it can be served in many delicious ways: fish cakes, fish loaf, creamed fish, and other dishes you can add to this list because you have eaten them yourself.

All over the world, people like to eat dried fish: shark

meat in Peru, shark fins in China, *torkfish* in Norway, sturgeon in Asia, abalone in Mexico, octopus and squid in the Mediterranean, shrimp in Louisiana, and of course, codfish in New England.

THAT SMOKY TASTE

Smoking is another way of drying that makes fish taste different and delicious. The first settlers in New England smoked their fish to be eaten during the long hard winter months. In the early days of our country, the smokehouse was an important part of every farm. It was a wooden building with a door but no windows. Its inside walls were black from years of smoking. The ceiling had heavy iron hooks, on which hams, bacon, and fish were hung. In the floor was the fire pit, where wood was burned with a low fire that sent up a steady smoke around the food.

Even today, fish are smoked in this way in Canada, Europe, and our own country. Some fish are cold-smoked, or light-smoked; others are hot-smoked, or barbecued. In cold-smoking, the fish are hung at some distance from the fire, and they seldom get hotter than 100 degrees Fahrenheit, about the temperature of a very hot summer day. In hot-smoking, the fish are hung closer to the fire; in that way they are smoked and cooked at the same time.

The modern smokehouse is a big warehouse room with brick walls, concrete floors, and blocked-up windows. The fire burns in a metal fire-pit at the bottom, while the smoke rises up and escapes through a skylight. The fish hang between the fire pit and the roof.

The smoke is made by burning sawdust and wood shavings. Many kinds of machinery control the amount of heat and smoke, and the moisture of the air in the smokehouse. Some kinds of wood are better than others because they give the fish special flavors and color. Hickory, oak, old apple wood, dead orange tree wood, and even corn cobs and leaf ribs are used.

Almost any kind of fish can be smoked. Herring, salmon, and haddock are the most popular, but bluefish, shad, butterfish, flounder, mackerel, halibut, catfish, eels, sturgeon, whitefish, and even shrimp are also smoked. Each has its own special taste, which appeals to different people. Hard or "red" smoked herring is a national dish in Scotland. Large, lightly smoked herring, called bloaters, are popular in the United States. Finnan haddie (smoked haddock) are eaten in England and in the United States. *Beleke* is dried, hard-smoked salmon, cured the way the Indians first did it in Alaska and is still used by the Eskimos. In Germany and the Netherlands, you will find smoked eels in many stores, but they are also eaten in our country.

SALTING TO KEEP

Salting has been used more than any other way of preserving fish. The fish are placed in vats in between layers of dry salt. The water from the bodies of the fish quickly wets the salt, until it turn to *brine*—a mixture of water and a lot of salt. At the same time, the fish soak up some of the salt. This changes their fresh, clear, soft flesh to firm, tough, drier meat, which will not spoil. In about two or three weeks, the salter says that the fish is "struck through," or cured. Twenty pounds of salt will cure about 100 pounds of fish. Salting will keep herring, mackerel, salmon, and other fat fish from spoiling for several years.

Sometimes fish that have been pickled or *kenched* in brine are also dried in the air afterwards. Much of the salt cod shipped to us from Canada is preserved by this salt drying. After they are "struck through," the fish are piled in stacks, or kenches, about three feet high, on wooden racks several inches above the floor. The weight of the fish is enough to press out some of the brine. Then they are spread out on wooden frames and dried in the open air.

Most of the newer fisheries don't depend on the open air for drying. Here the fish are placed on trays made of wooden frames covered with chicken wire in rooms like tunnels. The hot, dry air is blown in.

After all this, is the dried fish ready to eat? By no means. It is still "green-salted" or "wet-salted" fish. Next it is skinned and boned, unless it is sold to stores as "whole fish."

But even this is not all that can happen to a salted fish. The best fish, with the most meat, are piled up, cut into squares, and pressed into blocks. These fish "bricks" can be bought in a store or they may go on to still another factory. The rest is put through a machine that shreds it into small scraps and dries it even more. This is the flaked codfish you can buy for stew or chowder. But let's follow some of the fish flakes to another part of the fish factory.

FISH CAKES BY THE TON

Do you like fried fish cakes doused in tomato sauce? Of course, you can make them at home—and many people do—but you don't have to. In this part of the fish factory fish cakes are being fixed by the ton.

Flaked cod and peeled potatoes are cooked separately in huge boilers. After the cooked potatoes have been run through giant potato mashers, they are stirred together with the mashed, softened cod flakes until the two are thoroughly mixed together. Now the mixture is packed in air-tight cans. At home the fish-cake mixture is shaped into cakes, rolled in bread crumbs, and fried in deep fat in a frying pan. When you eat the fried fish cake much later, what does it taste like—fish or potato? Why, it's a special fish-cake taste, not like either one alone.

Preparation of fish cakes

Pots in which potatoes and fish are cooked separately
Mixing cooked fish and potatoes together
Fish cake mixture on its way to canning machine
Machine that fills the cans with fish-cake mixture
Sealed fish-cake cans in large wire basket are lowered into steamer where they are sterilized

ENTER CANNED FISH

For hundreds of years drying, smoking, salting and pickling were the only ways of preserving food. Then, about 150 years ago Nicholas Appert, a French candymaker, found that he could preserve food by cooking it in a corked glass container. When Peter Durand, an Englishman, made the first tin can, the eating habits of the whole world changed. A family in England could eat tuna caught in the Pacific. And salmon could be "in season" all the year round, even if it wasn't dried or salted.

Ten years ago, more than a third of all the fish caught in the United States waters reached the family kitchen in tin cans. It was ready to eat, because it was cooked before being "put up" in the cans. And it tasted very good.

Some fish, like shrimp and lobster, are simply boiled and seasoned before they are put into the cans. Fish roe and some bonita are packed in brine; tuna, salmon, sardines, and kippers are canned in oil. Some canned fish is smoked and salted, like sprats, anchovies, mussels, and

oysters. You can even get it in wine sauce or vinegar. What a lot of delicious new tastes!

Whatever the fish and however it is packed, the method of canning is the same. After the fish has been prepared and placed in the tin, the lid is sealed under high pressure in giant iron kettles. This forces all the air out of the can. Without air the bacteria cannot grow and spoil the fish. Those few kinds which can grow without air are destroyed by thorough boiling and cooking with steam under high pressure. This is the way your mother preserves food when she cans food in a pressure cooker. When you see the label *"vacuum sealed"* it means that all the air has been exhausted in giant pressure cookers, and the cans sealed in the absence of air. Then the fish is always good to eat, even years after it has been taken from the ocean.

FROZEN ON A SHELF

In your kitchen refrigerator you can keep left-over food for several days. Put a thermometer into the box, and you will find that the temperature is between 34 and 38 degrees. The newest refrigerators also have freezing compartments. Here you can keep food frozen stiff. As long as the vegetables, strawberries, fish, hamburgers, and even soups are frozen solid, they will stay good to eat almost indefinitely.

Preserving food by keeping it cold is very new in most parts of the world. In 1851, Dr. John Gorrie, an American, invented the first refrigerating machine. For the first time, food could be kept really cool in warm weather. Cool, and safe to eat.

But for many hundreds of years, Eskimos in the far north have had their own natural deep freezes. There the earth never really warms up. Dig down a few feet, and you hit frozen ground that never thaws. The Eskimos hacked out pits in this hard earth and kept their food there—cold and fresh. People in other parts of the world were not so lucky, until Dr. Gorrie's invention.

In a deep freezer today the temperature is kept at zero, whether it's in a frozen food locker, in the corner grocery store, or at home. Food wouldn't keep any better at the North Pole.

Frozen fish tastes more like fresh fish than any other kind of preserved fish. Freezing does not change the flavor, or make the flesh either harder or softer. More and more frozen fish is sold every year. It can be frozen

Quick freezers

whole or in fillets, in sticks or in cakes, raw or cooked.
You can buy frozen perch, halibut, swordfish, sole, lobster tails, mackerel, or cod from almost any part of the
world, in and out of season, any day of the year, and it
doesn't even have to be cleaned. Of course, frozen fish
costs more per pound, because a lot of work has gone
into it.

Sharp frozen, *deep* frozen, or *quick* frozen—people in
the food trade may use any of these words, but they all
mean the same thing: the food is frozen hard at a very
low temperature. Large, whole fish are frozen in a room
where the temperature is 5 to 7 degrees *below* zero. Then
it is raised to zero, and the fish will stay at this temperature until they are sold. At that time they are cut into
steak slices with a band saw, packed frozen in boxes,
delivered to the store in trucks equipped with freezing
machines, and sold in the store from freezers which are
equally cold.

You certainly don't want to stay very long in the
freezing room. The workers who go in and out wear
heavy clothes, ear muffs, and warm boots. Even so, they
stay inside for only a few minutes at a time, just long
enough to put in or take out the fish.

You can buy frozen fish in small packages that hold
two or three helpings. Some of it is frozen after it has
been made ready to cook; some of it is actually cooked
first, and then frozen. The small packages of fish are
placed on the shelves in freezing compartments that look
like large refrigerators. Their heavy doors are lined with
cork to keep out the warm air, so the temperature will

stay below zero. Many thousands of pounds of packaged fish are lined up on the shelves of the plant ready to be shipped frozen all the way to your table.

Your great-great-grandmother never dreamed of buying spring mackerel in December, and buying it already cooked at that! Nowadays you can buy frozen chowder, oyster stew, shrimp soup, fried shrimp, codfish cakes, fishburgers, fish sticks, and fish pies ready to heat and eat in a few minutes. These are the modern ways of buying fish: factory-cleaned, factory-cooked, and factory frozen.

THE NEWEST TASTE

Only a few years ago any Gloucester fisherman would have told you that the "bottom had fallen out" of the groundfish business. The fishermen were catching more cod, haddock, rosefish, and pollock than they could sell. There didn't seem to be enough people to eat all those fish. The fishermen were getting less and less pay for their work, and the fishery owners were worrying, because the price of fish was steadily falling. If only they could find a way to make people eat more fish! Something would have to be done, or the industry would "fold."

A new idea and an old machine did the trick. For years, the bakeries have used special machines for cooking doughnuts to a crisp, golden brown. Suppose the same thing was done to codfish? The idea was tried out, and the result was delicious! The fish-stick industry had arrived. 1953 is now known as "Fish Stick Year"—over seven million pounds of fish sticks were sold for a total of $4,000,000! By 1954, 50 million pounds of sticks were produced. Here was a big new market for part of the catch which had for years found no market at all.

Let's visit the fish-stick department of our fishery. In this room you can follow every step—from fish blocks to packaged sticks. As you can see, no fresh fish ever enters here. It arrives in the frozen blocks—mostly cod. After the blocks are unwrapped, a worker with an electric band saw cuts them into strips about five inches long. The next worker saws the strips into stick size—a half inch thick, three-quarters of an inch wide, and four inches long, and weighing one ounce. From here the sticks go to a conveyor belt covered with bread crumbs which stick to them because they are now thawed out a little. Then on through a batter of eggs and flour, then more bread crumbs. Now the sticks are ready for the "doughnut" machine. The belt drops them into a tank full of hot fat. When they are golden brown, they are

Electric saw cutting the frozen cod fish blocks into sticks (left). Fish sticks being breaded and entering fryer (right).

Fried fish sticks coming out of hot fat (left). Fish sticks being packed (right).

taken out on a belt, drained, and cooled on moving racks. The only thing left to do is to wrap and package them, ten to a box.

Every day thousands of these sealed packages are produced, kept for a while in a cooler, and then quick-frozen. When your mother buys them, she only has to heat them in the oven. Yum, yum, here is fish with a really new flavor, never tasted before 1953!

CHAPTER SEVEN

Sea Food—But Not Fish

The sea is rich with living creatures, and they are not all fish. What name would you give to oysters, clams, mussels, scallops, snails, or abalone? They are all soft-bodied animals, without a backbone, and covered with a hard shell. And they are all very good to eat. Scientists have a word for them: *molluscs*. But in the trade, they are called *shellfish* (along with lobsters, shrimps, and crabs). They are usually handled in special fisheries—"shellfisheries," you might call them.

OYSTERS—IN SEASON AND OUT

More oysters are caught than any other kind of shellfish. In fact, next to salmon, oysters are the most valuable of water "crops." Each year 100 million pounds of oysters are taken from North American waters. Almost all of this

Tongs for oysters

comes from the Middle and South Atlantic coast, and 35 million pounds come from Chesapeake Bay alone.

Oysters grow in almost any kind of clean water. But they get along best in shallow, quiet bays, or river mouths, where the sea water mixes with fresh water and is less salty. The oysters fasten themselves to rocky or muddy bottoms, to clean shells or other hard objects. Once they are "set," they never move away.

Oysters are living strainers. Through their gills they draw in great quantities of water, from which they strain out their food—all kinds of tiny plants and animals. An adult oyster can strain 25 quarts of water in one hour. How many billions of the tiny things does an oyster eat in a day?

Like clams and scallops, oysters are not "fished." They are dredged, dug, or scooped up by almost any gear that

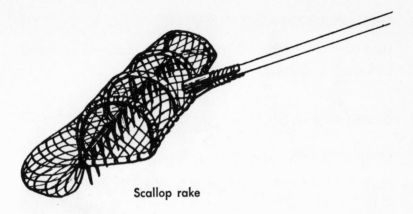

Scallop rake

will pry them loose. (You could hardly expect an oyster to bite at a hook!) Tongs, rakes, forks, hoes, and dredges are used (see picture on page 21).

A dredge is a shallow metal mesh bag with a heavy metal frame and a bar across the mouth of the frame. The short teeth on the frame scoop the oysters up from the bottom. Then there are jet dredges which have no teeth; instead they pry the oysters loose with a gushing stream of water and then scoop them up. The dredges are fastened by short tow lines to a pole laid across the boat that tows them along. Some of the larger boats have dredges mounted on revolving cranes. They can gather 25 bushels of oysters every 2 minutes!

For hundreds of years people have thought of oysters as something special. The Greeks and the Romans served them at their banquets. When the early settlers from Europe found that American shores teemed with oysters, they were delighted. What a fine, rich land!

And oysters *are* a wonderful food. Every bit is good to eat (except the shell, of course) and you can serve them in a dozen ways: raw on the half shell, cooked in stew or chowder, baked, fried, broiled, creamed, chopped and fried in fritters.

OYSTER TIME

OYSTERS R IN SEASON. You often see this sign in restaurants or fish markets. What does the "R" stand for? It is just a convenient way of reminding you that oysters *are* in season from September through April, the months with the letter "r" in their names. Does this mean that there aren't any oysters from May through August? No, but it does have something to do with the way oysters grow.

Oysters spawn in the summer. Each female may lay 500 million eggs in one season. Most of these eggs never grow into real oysters. Very few live long enough to "set" —on the shell, rock, or sea bottom. The oyster has many natural enemies: starfish, snails, crayfish, crabs, ghost shrimps, oyster leeches, ducks, and sponges. Out of the *hundreds of millions* of eggs laid by one female oyster, only *one or two* live to grow up. And growing up takes two to five years! No wonder oysters are so expensive.

During the summer spawning season, the oysters lose weight, get watery, and are not very good to eat. After a short rest they grow plump and tasty again. And there are two more reasons why we don't eat oysters in the months without "r." First, they spoil easily, especially in hot weather. Second, it is very important to give the young oysters a chance to grow. So the states have passed laws against taking oysters during the spawning season.

Of course, if you have plenty of money to spend in expensive restaurants, you can eat oysters any time. They are last year's but they are perfectly good to eat. By now you certainly know why: this year's crop is kept cold and fresh in the shell or frozen "shucked." Either way it can wait till next year to be eaten.

SHUCKING OYSTERS

Fresh oysters for dinner today! But how do you know they are fresh?

If you buy them in the shell, they must be alive. Otherwise they are not good to eat. How can you tell? Live oysters' shells are always tightly closed. An oyster has only one muscle—the one that opens and shuts its shell. Unless it is "set" and getting food this muscle pulls the shell tight shut. If it gapes open, you can be sure the oyster is dead, and no good for you.

You can also buy shucked (or shelled) oysters either fresh or frozen. There is a trick to shucking: after the oyster is thoroughly washed in cold water to wash off all the sand and mud, a special oyster knife is forced between the two halves of the shell at the thin end. The muscle that closes the shell is then cut where it is attached to the shells. That leaves the oyster loose in the deep part of the shell.

This is the way oysters are shucked at home or in your local fish market. But it's far too slow for canneries and shucking houses. There machines are used to grade, wash, shuck, and pack the oysters.

TESTED CLAMS

Clams don't taste like oysters, but they *are* like them in a lot of other ways. For one thing, they spoil easily. That's why the government and fisheries which sell their products in their own retail stores inspect shucked clams (and *all* shellfish) to make sure you get them fresh.

When clams are alive, they are cream colored; their flesh is firm and crisp. Sometimes they may look this way, but they aren't always fit to eat. There are laboratories where special workers check on their freshness in many ways.

Samples of the shucked clams are checked first for cleanliness: are they free from sand and pieces of shell? Then the clam juice is inspected for bacteria and the wastes they leave behind. Milk and water have gone through much the same tests for many years.

When the tests are finished, the laboratory worker grades, rejects or approves the clams. His report looks something like a school report card which tells how you are doing in various subjects.

A report on clams might say:

IDENTIFICATION:

Brand: Blue Star

Packer: Johnson & Wayne

Shipped: October 19, 1955

Analyzed: October 22, 1955

RESULTS OF ANALYSIS:

Weight: 24 gms. (a little less than an ounce)

Size: 1½ inches

Temperature on arrival: 38 degrees (If higher than 40 degrees, it is rejected)

Amount of liquor (juice): 4% (If more than 5%, it cannot be sold)

Bacteria: Kind   Number

Bacterial wastes: (If too much, the sample is discarded)

Pieces of shell: (*None* are allowed)

Then the clams (or other shellfish) are given a grade: 4, 3, 2, 1, or 0.

4 means excellent, 3 is good, 2 is fair; 1 is poor, and not fit to eat; 0 is the same as 1, only worse.

Like shellfish, packaged fish are also inspected. The laboratory checks for worms, bits of bone, bloodspots, skin or scales, and rejects or approves the samples. No matter what happens to a fish—whether it is filleted, frozen, canned, smoked, salted, or pickled—it must pass the test. You don't have to poke it and smell it to make sure it's good to eat. The laboratory does the job for you a lot better than you could do it for yourself.

CHAPTER EIGHT

The Fish You Don't Eat

How much of a fish can you eat? Bones—no. Scales and skin—no. Heads, fins, and tails—no. Insides—no. Why, that's more than a third of every fish. What happens to it all? It may not be food for you, but some of it does become food of another sort, and a lot is used in other ways. Also there are certain fish that are caught but never reach the dinner table at all. Let's go on and see what can happen to fish that isn't eaten.

FISH FOR BAIT

Fishermen work hard to catch certain kinds of fish that you never see in your local fish market. Have you ever seen *alewives* in a fish store? Probably not, but they are caught in eastern waters all the way from New England to Florida—mostly around Chesapeake Bay. In the spring the alewives swim up the rivers in huge schools during the day. At night they go back to the ocean, and then they are netted by the million. Only a very small part of this enormous catch is eaten fresh; the rest is salted and stored. For human food? No, for bait to catch more valuable fish.

Another member of the herring family, the *menhaden*, are also caught mainly off the Middle Atlantic states. (See picture on page 58.) The young, about 5 to 6 inches long and weighing only an ounce-and-a-half, are caught in bays and river mouths, where they come to feed after spawning out in the ocean.

When you go fishing, you often use minnows as bait for pickerel or bass. In the same way, salted alewives and menhaden are bait for red snapper in the Gulf of Mexico and tuna in the Pacific.

Eels are a good food fish, though they are not as popular as many others. The Italian people in our country buy eels for their main dish at Christmas Eve dinners, just as their families in Italy have done for centuries. And thousands of sport fishermen who catch eels know how good they taste—boiled, fried, baked or pickled. But the fisheries in the Middle Atlantic states don't sell them for food.

MORE MINK COATS

Fish are sold as food for birds and animals as well as people. In fact, without fish there wouldn't be so many mink coats. This sounds queer, but it is true. Mink are small, rat-like animals raised on "farms" or "ranches" for their beautiful fur. They live on fish. Barrels and barrels of waste fish are delivered to mink farms to feed the hungry little animals. It's inexpensive for the mink farmers, and the fisheries are glad to sell it.

If fish is good for mink, why not feed it to other animals or even birds? Poultry farmers either raise their own corn or buy grain and mash to feed their hens and chicks. In recent years grain prices went so high that the farmers could barely afford to stay in business. So they looked around for a cheaper feed. At the same time, the fisheries were hunting for other ways to get rid of their fish waste, and also part of the unsold catch. Why not feed it to chickens? But making fish into chicken feed is not as simple as shipping barrels of waste to a mink farm. Let's see how it's done at our fishery.

CHICKENS ON A FISH PIER

What on earth are hundreds of baby chicks doing in a fishery? This surprises us as much as anything we have seen on our visit. Come into the laboratory and find out, a white-coated worker invites us. Here the workers aren't handling fish at all! They're raising chickens, and not even for market. Instead scientists are using the chicks to try out different kinds of feed.

The laboratory man points out dozens of bottles containing different kinds of *fish meal*. This is waste fish ground into a brown powder which looks like grain mash.

Some meal is made from fat fish, some from lean. The scientists carefully mix them together in different ways. Which is best? That's where the live chicks come in. The laboratory workers watch them closely to see how fast they grow on one kind of meal or another, how fleshy they get, how many eggs the hens lay.

In this way they find out which feed will produce the best chickens at the lowest cost. And so the work of the scientist helps both the fisheries that want to sell their extra fish, and hen farmers who need cheaper and better chicken feed.

FROM OCEAN TO SOIL

Menhaden are used not as food for people but as food for the soil. Except for the roe, or eggs, these fish are ground up and shipped to far-off farms. Some of the fish meal will be used for chickens and hogs, but most of it will be spread on fields all over the country.

What good can fish meal possibly do on a plowed field? When the microscopic bacteria in the soil feed on it, they change it into chemicals that help plants to grow. In other words, fish meal is a fine fertilizer.

We don't eat waste fish, but it *does* help to feed us. It is used as bait to catch the fish we do eat. It is used as feed for the chickens we enjoy for Sunday dinner. It is used as fertilizer to grow vegetables that end up on our table. So fish are important to our diet in more ways than one!

A HUNDRED USES

Menhaden is a fatty fish and has lots of oil. The older fish (3 to 4 years old) are very valuable for this reason. About one fourth of all fish-oil in the United States comes from menhaden.

Every year hundreds of thousands of gallons are taken from menhaden and alewives. When the fish are steamed, the oil oozes out of the flesh. You won't find menhaden oil at the corner grocery store. Most of it ends up in factories. And how many different uses it has! It is made into soap and pet food; it is mixed with different colors to make paint and varnish; it goes into insect sprays and printing inks. It is also used in greasing all kinds of machinery, in finishing leather, and even in manufacturing aluminum and steel. This fish, which is too fat to eat, is important just because it *is* fat.

STICKY STUFF

Factories also use other parts of fish besides the oil: the skin, bladder, and bones, for instance. Almost next-door to many fisheries you will find glue factories. Here fish bones are crushed; the skin is steeped in lime and then boiled. The fat is removed by boiling in naphtha. This dissolves fat just the way cleaning fluid takes a grease stain out of your clothes.

The rest is cooked in steam under pressure. This dissolves out the sticky stuff from which mucilage and liquid glue are made.

VITAMINS FOR BABY

Have you had your vitamins today? Did the baby get his cod liver oil? If you eat enough of the right kind of food, you get nearly all the vitamins you need. All but one, that is. There just isn't enough Vitamin D in your regular food, especially in winter. Your baby brother or sister needs even more Vitamin D to grow strong, healthy bones and teeth. That's why your mother buys it in a bottle and feeds it to him, a few drops at a time. Look at the label on the bottle. Why, Vitamin D—and Vitamin A, too—come from fish liver. It may be codfish, or perhaps halibut, salmon, tuna, sablefish or even shark.

As you get older and don't grow so fast, you don't need to get these vitamins from fish liver oils. Many of your foods contain enough Vitamin A, and you can get enough Vitamin D in the summer, if you play a lot in the sun. Sunlight helps your body to make its own Vitamin D. But, you ask, how can you get Vitamin D from fish like cod and halibut, which never see the light of day in their deep ocean waters? Fish, too, need Vitamin D to live and grow. How do they get along without sunlight? Their livers can store lots of Vitamin D out of the food the fish eat. Lucky for us that they can!

Nowadays scientists have learned how to get the oil from livers and vitamins from the oil. Drug companies can now bottle it and sell it.

What happens to the "waste" parts of a fish? They are all used! Look at the list below and see.

FLESH: food for people.

OILS in factories for paint, soap and grease.
SCRAPS: fish meal for animals and fertilizer for soil.
BONES and SKIN: glue.
LIVER OILS: vitamins.
SCALES: "pearl" buttons.

CHAPTER NINE

Fish in the Future

NEW WAYS OF FISHING

The fishing industry has traveled a long way since the days of *Captains Courageous* fifty years ago. Fishing is not so dangerous any more. Dory fishing is almost gone. Powerful Diesel-engined draggers make two trips a month and easily bring in 100,000 pounds of fish each time. These sea-going giants make our *Nancy Lee* look almost like a toy.

Gone, too, are most of the ship owners with one or two small boats. The great trawlers and seiners of today are owned mainly by large companies that also run big fisheries on shore. These companies have their own docks, ships, machinery, freezing and canning factories, warehouses, and fleets of trucks. The smaller, old-time boats and fisheries cannot keep up with them.

Today fish are prepared for market in new ways. Much less fresh and cured fish is sold today. Many more tons of fish are sold frozen in supermarkets and groceries than fresh in neighborhood fish stores. Fish come to your table from huge factories like the ones that bake bread and cake, pack meat, or can fruit and vegetables. Fishing is now a big industry, and both the skipper of the *Nancy Lee* and the foreman of the fish-stick factory know it.

There isn't much "waste" fish any more. It is now turned into fish oils, fish meal, fertilizer, oleomargarine, medicine, vitamins and even a kind of "egg white," which is dried and sold by the pound. And some of the waste leaves the fishery for other factories to be made into glue, paint, and many other useful things.

FISH SCIENCE

Does this mean that we have learned all we need to know about fishing? Are we doing everything we can to harvest the ocean crop? No, fish scientists will tell you, we have only just begun. Have we caught nearly all the fish in many places close to shore and on the banks? There are still countless new fishing grounds to be discovered. The vast oceans are teeming with fish we don't even know about. The scientist says that we are still "hunting" fish the way stone-age people hunted wild animals, and gathered wild fruits and berries. We still catch the fish where we find them. We have hardly started to "farm" the ocean—to *produce* fish when and where we want them, the way we produce cattle and chickens, grain, fruit, and vegetables.

But we *have* learned new and better ways of finding, catching, preparing, and preserving fish. And we have learned a great deal about the ocean itself.

Oceanographers—scientists who explore the ocean—have changed the fish "maps" so much that the old-timers wouldn't recognize them. They have discovered all kinds of new places where fish live in huge quantities. They have learned about the deepest parts of the oceans, not only hundreds but thousands of miles from shore. A new instrument called the *sea scanner* has taken most of the guesswork out of fishing. It helps the fishermen find fish half a mile away in any direction—even straight down. The sea scanner sends out sounds that bounce around the ocean and send back echoes from the places where there are lots of fish. Then the scanner picks up these return signals, and men trained to recognize them can tell where the fish are, and even what kinds of fish they are!

S. O. S. FOR FISH

Other scientists are studying the fish diseases which kill millions of fish every year. One such disease—"red tide"—is caused by tiny ocean plants and animals which poison the fish with the wastes they leave in the water. At times the red water reaches a hundred miles out from shore, and the dead fish are washed up on the beaches in piles several feet high. Much more work needs to be done to stop this wholesale destruction of our fish crop.

What can be done to save the oysters, to cut down

the number of those destroyed before they have a chance to grow up? Ways have already been found to "farm" oysters by growing them in safe places and "planting" them in clean shells.

Many fish are being destroyed by big dams which supply more water for people and farms. On the West Coast, some of those dams are built across the large rivers, where the salmon come each year. The fish cannot find the way back to places where they lay their eggs. So fish "ladders" are built beside the dams. The salmon can leap up the ladders and past the dams to finish their long journey.

Other rivers are filled with silt and sand which choke the fish. Fish die in still others because wastes from city factories poison the water.

How can we save all these valuable fish? Both na-

Fish ladder

tional and state governments have made a beginning. Silt is being removed from some rivers. Laws have been passed that require city wastes to be dumped out in the ocean instead of into the rivers. Other laws set the seasons when certain fish may be caught. Laws also say how large the mesh size of the nets must be. To save the young haddock, New England laws require that the mesh in the cod end of the net cannot be smaller than 4½ inches. This lets the smaller fish get out through the holes and grow until they are old enough to lay eggs. Young fish in streams are marked with metal tags with a number, and with directions for returning them to the right laboratory. There scientists keep cards with the same number and records that tell their "birth" date, their original weight and age, and where they were first tagged. Only fish of a certain age, length, and weight can be kept when they are caught.

MORE FISH TO EAT

In England, Norway, and on our Pacific coast, floating fish factories sail out beyond the banks to deeper waters. There the fish are caught, cleaned, and frozen right on the ship!

All of these changes mean more fish for people to eat. So the government helps by teaching people more and better ways to use fish. Books are printed that explain how to buy and cook shrimp, clams, rosefish, hake, whiting and other less used fish. If you want to learn how to make some very nice fish dishes, you can follow the recipes in books published by the government, which you can get by writing to the Department of the Interior, Washington, D.C.

Government scientists and fish experts will tell you that the ocean is still "wide open." It is a frontier where much of the food of the future will some day be claimed by the people of all the world.

When we started out, we thought we were just going to a fish pier, but we've done a lot of traveling. We have gone to the Banks and up into Chesapeake Bay. We've been to the Pacific Coast and out into the open ocean. We have visited the *Nancy Lee* and we have seen factories and even a laboratory. We have talked with fishermen, fishery workers, and scientists. We have even gone back in history to see how people fished in ancient times and how the Gloucester fishermen brought in the catch a hundred years ago. We have seen how much work has to be done before a fish ends up on our dinner table.